First World War
and Army of Occupation
War Diary
France, Belgium and Germany

49 DIVISION
146 Infantry Brigade
Prince of Wales's Own (West Yorkshire Regiment)
1/8th Battalion
14 April 1915 - 31 December 1917

WO95/2795/2

The Naval & Military Press Ltd
www.nmarchive.com
Published in association with The National Archives

Published by

The Naval & Military Press Ltd

Unit 10 Ridgewood Industrial Park,
Uckfield, East Sussex,
TN22 5QE England
Tel: +44 (0) 1825 749494

www.naval-military-press.com

www.nmarchive.com

This diary has been reprinted in facsimile from the original. Any imperfections are inevitably reproduced and the quality may fall short of modern type and cartographic standards.

© **Crown Copyright**
Images reproduced by permission of The National Archives, London, England, 2015.

Contents

Document type	Place/Title	Date From	Date To
Heading	WO95/2795/2 1/8 Battalion West Yorkshire Regiment.		
Miscellaneous	49th Division 146th Infy Bde. 1-8th Bn West Yorks Regt. Apr 1915-Dec 1917. 62 Div. 185 Bde.		
Heading	146th Inf. Bde. 49th Div. Battn. disembarked Boulogne from England 16.4.15. 1/8th Battn. The West Yorkshire Regiment. April (14/30.4.15) 1915-Nov 17		
War Diary	Gainsborough (Lincolnshire)	14/04/1915	14/04/1915
Miscellaneous	Gainsborough	15/04/1915	15/04/1915
War Diary	Boulogne	16/04/1915	16/04/1915
War Diary	Pont Debrique	17/04/1915	17/04/1915
War Diary	Merville	17/04/1915	22/04/1915
War Diary	La Gorgue	23/04/1915	30/04/1915
Heading	146th Inf. Bde. 49th Div. 1/8th Battn. The West Yorkshire Regiment. May 1915		
War Diary	La Gorgue	01/05/1915	02/05/1915
War Diary	Bac St. Maur	03/05/1915	04/05/1915
War Diary	Cameron Lane (M.21.b)	05/05/1915	05/05/1915
War Diary	M.21.b.	06/05/1915	08/05/1915
War Diary	M.22.c 3000 S. Of Lavantie	09/05/1915	09/05/1915
War Diary	M.22.c	10/05/1915	10/05/1915
War Diary	M.22.d.	11/05/1915	15/05/1915
War Diary	Lavantie	16/05/1915	17/05/1915
War Diary	G.31.c.	18/05/1915	18/05/1915
War Diary	Rue Du Quesnoy	19/05/1915	27/05/1915
War Diary	Rue Quesnoy	28/05/1915	30/05/1915
War Diary	Le Trou	31/05/1915	31/05/1915
War Diary	Rue Petillion	31/05/1915	31/05/1915
Heading	146th Inf. Bde. 49th Div. 1/8th Battn. The West Yorkshire Regiment. June 1915		
War Diary	Le Trou	01/06/1915	05/06/1915
War Diary	Rue Quesnoy	06/06/1915	11/06/1915
War Diary	Le Trou	12/06/1915	17/06/1915
War Diary	Rue Quesnoy	18/06/1915	23/06/1915
War Diary	Le Trou	24/06/1915	25/06/1915
War Diary	1/2 mile N. of Doulieu	27/06/1915	27/06/1915
War Diary	N. of Doulieu	28/06/1915	28/06/1915
War Diary	1 mile S. of Fletre	29/06/1915	29/06/1915
War Diary	Proven	30/06/1915	30/06/1915
Heading	146th Inf. Bde. 49th Div. 1/8th Battn. The West Yorkshire Regiment. July 1915. Attached: Appendix "A".		
War Diary	2 M. S.E. of Elverdinghe	01/07/1915	04/07/1915
War Diary	Chateau Elverdinghe	05/07/1915	07/07/1915
War Diary	Chateau Des Trois Tours	08/07/1915	13/07/1915
War Diary	C.14.D.1.1. (Sheet 28)	14/07/1915	19/07/1915
War Diary	Canal Bank	20/07/1915	25/07/1915
War Diary	C.14.D.1.1 Sheet 28	26/07/1915	27/07/1915
War Diary	C.14.D.1.1	28/07/1915	31/07/1915
Heading	Appendix "A"		
Miscellaneous	Distribution of Infantry. Appendix A.		

Miscellaneous	11th Infantry Brigade Coy No. 16. Appx A.	03/07/1915	03/07/1915
Diagram etc	Communications 11th Bde. Appendix B.		
Operation(al) Order(s)	Operation Order No. 1 by Brig-Genl C.B. Prowse Comdg. 11th Infantry Bde.	03/07/1915	03/07/1915
Diagram etc	This sketch is not to be taken into fire trenches. Appendix C.		
Miscellaneous		05/07/1915	05/07/1915
Miscellaneous			
Miscellaneous		04/07/1915	04/07/1915
Heading	146th Inf. Bde. 49th Div. 1/8th Battn. The West Yorkshire Regiment. August 1915		
War Diary	Trois Tours (Near Breilan)	01/08/1915	01/08/1915
War Diary	Trois Tours	02/08/1915	06/08/1915
War Diary	Sheet C.14.c.9.3	07/08/1915	12/08/1915
War Diary	Canal Bank	13/08/1915	13/08/1915
War Diary	Sheet 28 C.13.d.9.3	15/08/1915	24/08/1915
War Diary	Elverdinghe	25/08/1915	30/08/1915
War Diary	Sheet 28 C.13.d.4.3	31/08/1915	31/08/1915
Heading	146th Inf. Bde. 49th Div. 1/8th Battn. The West Yorkshire Regiment. September 1915		
War Diary	C.14.c.1.2	01/09/1915	04/09/1915
War Diary	Canal Bank	05/09/1915	09/09/1915
War Diary	A.16.a	10/09/1915	20/09/1915
War Diary	C.13.b.3.2	21/09/1915	26/09/1915
War Diary	Canal Bank	26/09/1915	30/09/1915
Heading	146th Inf. Bde. 49th Div. 1/8th Battn. The West Yorkshire Regiment. October 1915		
War Diary	Canal Bank	01/10/1915	02/10/1915
War Diary	C.13.b.3.3	03/10/1915	08/10/1915
War Diary	Canal Bank	09/10/1915	14/10/1915
War Diary	Coppernollehoek	16/10/1915	21/10/1915
War Diary	C.21.c 2.4	22/10/1915	24/10/1915
War Diary	Canal Bank	25/10/1915	27/10/1915
War Diary	C.21.d.4.4	29/10/1915	29/10/1915
War Diary	C.20.d.4.4	30/10/1915	31/10/1915
Heading	146th Inf. Bde. 49th Div. 1/8th Battn. The West Yorkshire Regiment. November 1915		
War Diary	C.20.d.4.4	01/11/1915	02/11/1915
War Diary	Canal Bank	03/11/1915	05/11/1915
War Diary	S.15.b.	06/11/1915	06/11/1915
Miscellaneous	C.21.c.4.2 1/2	07/11/1915	07/11/1915
War Diary	Belle Alliance	08/11/1915	09/11/1915
War Diary	Canal Bank	10/11/1915	11/11/1915
War Diary	C.21.c.4.2 1/2	12/11/1915	12/11/1915
War Diary	Belle Alliance	13/11/1915	14/11/1915
War Diary	Brielen	15/11/1915	17/11/1915
War Diary	Canal Bank	18/11/1915	19/11/1915
War Diary	A.8.b.1.5	20/11/1915	27/11/1915
War Diary	Elverdinghe	28/11/1915	30/11/1915
War Diary	Canal Bank	30/11/1915	30/11/1915
Heading	146th Inf. Bde. 49th Div. 1/8th Battn. The West Yorkshire Regiment. December 1915		
War Diary	Canal Bank	01/12/1915	03/12/1915
War Diary	Elverdinghe	04/12/1915	05/12/1915
War Diary	B.20.d.4.4	06/12/1915	09/12/1915
War Diary	Elverdinghe	10/12/1915	11/12/1915

War Diary	Canal Bank	12/12/1915	13/12/1915
War Diary	A.8.b.1.5	14/12/1915	21/12/1915
War Diary	B.20.d.4.4	22/12/1915	23/12/1915
War Diary	Canal Bank	24/12/1915	27/12/1915
War Diary	Elverdinghe	28/12/1915	29/12/1915
War Diary	Camp A.30	30/12/1915	30/12/1915
War Diary	Camp L.3	31/12/1915	31/12/1915
War Diary	Houtkerque	01/01/1916	01/01/1916
War Diary	Wormhoudt	02/01/1916	15/01/1916
War Diary	Millain	16/01/1916	16/01/1916
War Diary	Zutkerque	17/01/1916	17/01/1916
War Diary	Calais	18/01/1916	01/02/1916
War Diary	Fourdrinoy	02/02/1916	05/02/1916
War Diary	Breilly	06/02/1916	09/02/1916
War Diary	Molliens-Au-Bois	10/02/1916	10/02/1916
War Diary	Bouzincourt	11/02/1916	11/02/1916
War Diary	Front Line Trenches	12/02/1916	12/02/1916
War Diary	In Trenches	13/02/1916	20/02/1916
War Diary	In Support Authville, Etc.	21/02/1916	24/02/1916
War Diary	In Trenches	25/02/1916	29/02/1916
War Diary	Martinsart	01/03/1916	03/03/1916
War Diary	Varennes	04/03/1916	15/03/1916
War Diary	Beaucourt	16/03/1916	27/03/1916
War Diary	Bavelincourt	28/03/1916	31/03/1916
Heading	1/8 W York Regt Vol 8. April 1916		
War Diary	Bavelincourt	01/04/1916	07/04/1916
War Diary	Esbart	08/04/1916	08/04/1916
War Diary	Vignacourt	09/04/1916	30/04/1916
War Diary	Bavelincourt	01/04/1916	07/04/1916
War Diary	Esbart	08/04/1916	08/04/1916
War Diary	Vignacourt	09/04/1916	30/04/1916
War Diary	Vignacourt	01/05/1916	31/05/1916
Heading	146th Brigade. 49th Division. 1/8th Battalion West Yorkshire Regiment. June 1916		
War Diary	Herissart	01/06/1916	01/06/1916
War Diary	Aveluy Wood	02/06/1916	22/06/1916
War Diary	Herissart	23/06/1916	29/06/1916
War Diary	Varennes	30/06/1916	30/06/1916
Heading	146th Inf. Bde. 49th Div. War Diary 1/8th Battn. The West Yorkshire Regiment. July 1916		
War Diary	Theipval Wood	01/07/1916	02/07/1916
War Diary	Aveluy Wood	03/07/1916	03/07/1916
War Diary	Martinsart Wood	04/07/1916	07/07/1916
War Diary	Wood Post	08/07/1916	15/07/1916
War Diary	Lepzig	16/07/1916	17/07/1916
War Diary	Bluff	18/07/1916	19/07/1916
War Diary	Lepzig	20/07/1916	23/07/1916
War Diary	Bouzincourt	24/07/1916	27/07/1916
War Diary	Forceville	28/07/1916	31/07/1916
Heading	146th Brigade 49th Division. 1/8th Battalion West Yorkshire Regiment. August 1916		
War Diary	Quarry Post	01/08/1916	05/08/1916
War Diary	Glovcester Post	06/08/1916	15/08/1916
War Diary	Martinsart Wood	16/08/1916	17/08/1916
War Diary	Lealvillers	18/08/1916	27/08/1916
War Diary	Gordon Castle	28/08/1916	29/08/1916

War Diary	Hedauville	30/08/1916	31/08/1916
Heading	146th. Infantry Brigade 49th. Division 1/8th. West Yorkshire Regt. September 1916		
War Diary	Hedauville	01/09/1916	02/09/1916
War Diary	Aveluy	03/09/1916	03/09/1916
War Diary	Forceville	04/09/1916	18/09/1916
War Diary	Hedauville	19/09/1916	20/09/1916
War Diary	Belfast Wood	27/09/1916	27/09/1916
War Diary	Mailly Maillet	29/09/1916	29/09/1916
War Diary	Raincheval	30/09/1916	30/09/1916
War Diary	Halloy	01/10/1916	01/10/1916
War Diary	Humbercourt	11/10/1916	11/10/1916
War Diary	Humbercamp	18/10/1916	18/10/1916
War Diary	Bienvillers	24/10/1916	24/10/1916
War Diary	Fonquevillers	01/11/1916	02/11/1916
War Diary	St Amand	03/11/1916	08/11/1916
War Diary	Fonquevillers	09/11/1916	14/11/1916
War Diary	Bienvillers	15/11/1916	19/11/1916
War Diary	Fonquevillers	20/11/1916	25/11/1916
War Diary	Souastre	26/11/1916	30/11/1916
Heading	War Diary of 1/8th Batt. West Yorks Regt for December 1916. Vol 16		
War Diary	Souastre	01/12/1916	02/12/1916
War Diary	Fonquevillers	03/12/1916	05/12/1916
War Diary	Pas	06/12/1916	06/12/1916
War Diary	Le Souich	07/12/1916	31/12/1916
Heading	War Diary of 1/8th Batt. West Yorks Regt. for January 1917. Vol 17		
Heading	War Diary. of For 1917		
War Diary	Le Souich	01/01/1917	07/01/1917
War Diary	Bailleulmont	07/01/1917	10/01/1917
War Diary	Bailleulmont	09/01/1917	11/01/1917
War Diary	Trenches	11/01/1917	15/01/1917
War Diary	Bailleulval	15/01/1917	18/01/1917
War Diary	Bailleulval Trenches	19/01/1917	23/01/1917
War Diary	Bailleulmont	23/01/1917	26/01/1917
War Diary	Bailleulmont	25/01/1917	27/01/1917
War Diary	Trenches	27/01/1917	31/01/1917
War Diary	Bailleulval	31/01/1917	31/01/1917
Heading	War Diary of 1/8th Batt. West Yorks Regt for February 1917. Vol 18		
War Diary	Bailleulval	01/02/1917	28/02/1917
Heading	War Diary of 1/8th Batt West Yorks Regt for March 1917. Vol 1917		
Miscellaneous	Valle Chapelle and Trenches	01/03/1917	01/03/1917
War Diary	Trenches	02/03/1917	07/03/1917
War Diary	Laventie	07/03/1917	12/03/1917
War Diary	Laventie and Trenches	13/03/1917	13/03/1917
War Diary	Trenches	14/03/1917	19/03/1917
War Diary	Support Red House and Laventie	19/03/1917	20/03/1917
War Diary	Red House and Laventie	21/03/1917	24/03/1917
War Diary	Trenches	25/03/1917	30/03/1917
War Diary	Trenches Laventie	31/03/1917	31/03/1917
Heading	War Diary of 1/8th Batt West York Regt for April 1917. Vol 20		
War Diary	Laventie	01/04/1917	05/04/1917

War Diary	Laventie and Trenches M 24.3 to N 13.2	06/04/1917	06/04/1917
War Diary	Trenches	07/04/1917	08/04/1917
War Diary	Trenches M 24.3 to N 13.2	08/04/1917	11/04/1917
War Diary	In Support	12/04/1917	17/04/1917
War Diary	Trenches M 24.3 to N 13.2	18/04/1917	23/04/1917
War Diary	Trenches M 24.3 to N 13.2 and Laventie	24/04/1917	29/04/1917
War Diary	Trenches	30/04/1917	30/04/1917
War Diary	Trenches M 24.3 to N 13.2	30/04/1917	30/04/1917
War Diary	Laventie	27/04/1917	30/04/1917
War Diary	Trenches M.24.d.10.50 to N.13.c.42.58	01/05/1917	06/05/1917
War Diary	Support H.Q. at M.6.d.2.1	07/05/1917	11/05/1917
War Diary	Trenches N.13.c.42.58-N.8.d.05.85	12/05/1917	17/05/1917
War Diary	Trenches N.13.c.42.58 to N.8.d.05.85 Laventie	18/05/1917	20/05/1917
War Diary	Laventie	20/05/1917	24/05/1917
War Diary	Support Red House	24/05/1917	29/05/1917
War Diary	Laventie	30/05/1917	31/05/1917
Operation(al) Order(s)	Appendix. A. to 146 Inf Bde O.O. No. 48. Left Group R.F.A. Orders.		
Miscellaneous	Rates of Fire. 18-Pounders.		
Operation(al) Order(s)	146th Infantry Brigade-Operation Order No. 48. Appendix A.	06/05/1917	06/05/1917
Operation(al) Order(s)	Operation Order No. 20 by Major. S.S. Sykes, M.C. Commanding. 1/8th. West Yorkshire Regiment. Appendix B.	07/05/1917	07/05/1917
Miscellaneous	1/5th Bn. W. York. R. Appendix C.	04/05/1917	04/05/1917
Miscellaneous	Examination of Prisoner of 262 R.R., 79th. Res. Div. Captured in Fauquissart Sector. 7/5/17	07/05/1917	07/05/1917
Miscellaneous	Report on the examination of a wounded prisoner of the Ii Battn., 262nd Res. Inf. Regt., 79th Res. Div., captured on the night of 1/8th May during a raid on the enemy's trenches in m.24.d. (Sheet 36). Appendix E.		
Heading	War Diary of 1/8th Batt. West Yorks Regt. for June. 1917. Vol 22		
War Diary	Laventie	01/06/1917	04/06/1917
War Diary	Laventie and Trenches M.24.c.55.17 to N.13c.40.58	05/06/1917	07/06/1917
War Diary	Trenches M.24.c.55.17 to N.13.c.40.58	08/06/1917	08/06/1917
War Diary	Laventie	09/06/1917	09/06/1917
War Diary	Support (H.Q. M.6.d.2.1.)	10/06/1917	13/06/1917
War Diary	Trenches M.24.c.55.17 to N.13.c.40.58	13/06/1917	17/06/1917
War Diary	Laventie	18/06/1917	23/06/1917
War Diary	Temple Bar Trenches	24/06/1917	29/06/1917
War Diary	Temple Bar	30/06/1917	30/06/1917
Operation(al) Order(s)	Operation Order No. 32 by Lieut-Col. R.A. Hudson, D.S.O.- Commanding:- 1/8th. West Yorkshire Regt.	16/06/1917	16/06/1917
Operation(al) Order(s)	Operation Order No. 33. by Lieut-Col. R.A. Hudson, D.S.O.- Commanding. 1/8th. West Yorkshire Regt.	22/06/1917	22/06/1917
Operation(al) Order(s)	Operation Order No. 33. by Lieut-Col. R.A. Hudson, D.S.O.- Comdg. 1/8th. Bn. West Yorkshire Regt. Appendix C.	25/06/1917	25/06/1917
Heading	War Diary of 1/8th Batt. West Yorks Regt for July 1917. Vol 23		
War Diary	Red House M.6.d.2.1. Rubers 36 S.W.	01/07/1917	05/07/1917
War Diary	Tremple Bar	06/07/1917	09/07/1917
War Diary	Le Nouveau Monde	10/07/1917	13/07/1917
War Diary	Fort Mardycke	14/07/1917	15/07/1917
War Diary	Zuydecoote	16/07/1917	16/07/1917

War Diary	Coxyde	17/07/1917	18/07/1917
War Diary	Nieuport	18/07/1917	21/07/1917
War Diary	R.35.d (Belgium Sheet 11 S.E.)	23/07/1917	24/07/1917
War Diary	Oost Dunkerke	24/07/1917	24/07/1917
War Diary	Ribaillet Camp R.35.d. (Belgium Sheet 11 S.E.)	24/07/1917	31/07/1917
Heading	War Diary of 1/8th Batt West York Regt for August 1917. Vol 24		
War Diary	Ribaillet Camp Nr. Coxyde	01/08/1917	01/08/1917
War Diary	Coxyde	02/08/1917	02/08/1917
War Diary	Ghyvelde D.21.b. (Sheet 19 Belgium & France)	03/08/1917	05/08/1917
War Diary	Teteghem	05/08/1917	12/08/1917
War Diary	Fort De Dunes C.16.a (Sheet 19 Belgium and France)	12/08/1917	27/08/1917
War Diary	Fort De Dunes C.16.a	28/08/1917	28/08/1917
War Diary	Ghyvelde D.21.b. (Sheet 19 Belgium & France)	31/08/1917	31/08/1917
War Diary	War Diary of 1/8th Batt West York Regt for September 1917. Vol 25		
War Diary		23/09/1917	23/09/1917
War Diary		02/09/1917	17/09/1917
War Diary		10/09/1917	27/09/1917
War Diary	Neordpegne	28/09/1917	28/09/1917
War Diary	Tatinghem	30/09/1917	30/09/1917
Heading	War Diary of 1/6th West Yorkshire Rgt. for 1st to 31st October 1917		
War Diary	Tatinghem	01/10/1917	05/10/1917
War Diary	O.29.b.0.8	02/10/1918	03/10/1918
War Diary	L.8.D	05/10/1918	05/10/1918
War Diary	Vlamertinghe	07/10/1918	09/10/1918
War Diary	Attack West of Passchendable	09/10/1917	11/10/1917
War Diary	Vlamertinghe	12/10/1917	12/10/1917
War Diary	Winniezele	13/10/1917	28/10/1917
War Diary	Steenvoorde E.	29/10/1917	31/10/1917
Operation(al) Order(s)	146th Infantry Brigade Operation Order No. 73. Appendix A.	30/09/1917	30/09/1917
Miscellaneous	March Table to accompany 146th Infantry Brigade Operation Order No. 73		
Operation(al) Order(s)	146th Infantry Brigade Operation order No. 74. Appendix B (1)		
Miscellaneous	March Table to accompany 146th Infantry Brigade Operation Order No. 74		
Operation(al) Order(s)	1/8th. Bn. West Yorkshire Regiment Operation Order No. 48. Appendix B (ii).	02/10/1917	02/10/1917
Operation(al) Order(s)	1/8th. Bn. West Yorkshire Regiment Operation Order No. 75. Appendix C.	05/10/1917	05/10/1917
Miscellaneous	Attack West of Passchendaele. 146th Infantry Brigade Instructions No. 1. Appendix D.	05/10/1917	05/10/1917
Miscellaneous	Attack West of Passchendaele. 146th Infantry Brigade Instructions No. 2	05/10/1917	05/10/1917
Miscellaneous	2nd Anzac Artillery Instructions No. 12. Arrangements for S.O.S.	03/10/1917	03/10/1917
Map	146th Inf Brigade Map No 25		
Miscellaneous	Attack West of Passchendaele. 146th Infantry Brigade Instructions No. 3		
Miscellaneous	Attack West of Passchendaele. 146th Infantry Brigade Instructions No. 4	07/10/1917	07/10/1917
Miscellaneous	146th Infantry Brigade Administrative Instructions No. 1	07/10/1917	07/10/1917

Miscellaneous	Casualties-1/8th Bn. West Yorkshire Regiment. Appendix E.	09/10/1917	09/10/1917
Miscellaneous	146th Infantry Brigade Operation Order No. 78. Appendix F.	11/10/1917	11/10/1917
Miscellaneous	1/8th Bn. West Yorkshire Regiment. Operation Order No. 43. Appendix G.	27/10/1917	27/10/1917
Heading	War Diary November 1917. 1/8 West Yorkshire Regt. Vol 27		
War Diary	Steenvoorde	01/11/1917	09/11/1917
War Diary	H.24.c.4.4	10/11/1917	11/11/1917
War Diary	J.9.a.5.3	12/11/1917	15/11/1917
War Diary	J.4.a.8.6	16/11/1917	19/11/1917
War Diary	I.15.c.2.6	20/11/1917	20/11/1917
War Diary	H.27.b.3.6	21/11/1917	24/11/1917
War Diary	H.23.b.6.9	25/11/1917	28/11/1917
War Diary	I.13.b.2.9	28/11/1917	30/11/1917
Heading	War Diary 1/8th West Yorkshire Regiment. Vol 28		
War Diary	Infantry Barracks Ypres	01/12/1917	05/12/1917
War Diary	Garter Pt.	06/12/1917	11/12/1917
War Diary	Barracks	12/12/1917	12/12/1917
War Diary	Vancouver Camp	13/12/1917	17/12/1917
War Diary	Dragoon Camp	18/12/1917	28/12/1917
War Diary	Chateau Belge	29/12/1917	31/12/1917

WO95/2795/2
1/8 Battalion West Yorkshire Regiment

49TH DIVISION
146TH INFY BDE

1-8TH BN WEST YORKS REGT.
DFC
APR 1915- 1917

62 DIV 185 BDE

146th Inf.Bde.
49th Div.

Battn. disembarked
Boulogne from
England 16.4.15.

1/8th BATTN. THE WEST YORKSHIRE REGIMENT.

A P R I L

(14/30.4.15)

1 9 1 5

Army Form C. 2118.

WAR DIARY
or
INTELLIGENCE SUMMARY.
(Erase heading not required.)

Instructions regarding War Diaries and Intelligence Summaries are contained in F. S. Regs., Part II. and the Staff Manual respectively. Title pages will be prepared in manuscript.

Hour, Date, Place	Summary of Events and Information	Remarks and references to Appendices
8.20 a.m. 14th April 1915 GAINSBOROUGH (LINCOLNSHIRE)	Machine Gun Section, Transport section, 3 officers, 96 rank & file left for SOUTHAMPTON under command of Capt LONGBOTTOM en route for HAVRE	Victoria Sno Capt Byl
6.5 & 6.35 P.M 15th April 1915 GAINSBOROUGH	The Batt.n (less the above party) under command of Major J.W. ALEXANDER T.D. left in two trains for FOLKESTONE en route for BOULOGNE Total strength of Batt.n at this date:- 30 Officers, 1007 other ranks, 74 horses & mules, 2 M. Guns, 13 limbered wagons 6 G.S. wagons, 2 water carts, 1 medical cart	
2. A.M 16th April 1915 - BOULOGNE	Disembarked & proceeded to standing camp.	
11.45 P.M 16th April BOULOGNE	Marched from camp to entrain at PONT DE BRIQUE	
2.30 A.M 17th April PONT DE BRIQUE	Entrained 9 oclock train conveying the party under Capt LONGBOTTOM	
10.40 A.M 17th April MERVILLE	Detrained and went into billets	
18th April MERVILLE	In Billets. Route march	
19th April MERVILLE	C.O. with commanders & sergeants of right platoons, 3 subalterns & CSM 3 M - CSM trenches near FAUQUISSART for instruction with BEDFORD REGT for 24 hours	

(73989) W4141-463. 400,000. 9/14. H.&J.Ltd. Forms/C. 2118/10. Billets

Army Form C. 2118.

WAR DIARY
or
INTELLIGENCE SUMMARY.
1/9 West Yorkshire Regt
(Erase heading not required.)

Instructions regarding War Diaries and Intelligence Summaries are contained in F.S. Regs., Part II. and the Staff Manual respectively. Title pages will be prepared in manuscript.

Hour, Date, Place	Summary of Events and Information	Remarks and references to Appendices
20th April 1915 MERVILLE	A Coyt with commanders & Sergeants of left platoon with C.P.M.S. & Q.M.S. proceeded to FAUQUISSART for instruction in trenches with Bedfords Regt for 24 hours. Remainder in billets & training.	
21st April 1915 MERVILLE	Senior major with specialists proceeded to trenches for instruction with Scots Guards	
4.30 PM 22nd April 1915 MERVILLE	Marched to LA GORGUE attached to VIII Division Took over Truck billets	
23rd April 1915 LAGORGUE	In billets. Two platoons sent to trenches for instruction with 2/o Bde	
24th April 1915 LAGORGUE	In billets	
25th April 1915 LAGORGUE	In billets. Two platoons (1 & 2) sent to trenches for inoculation with the 20th Bde	
26th April LAGORGUE	In billets. No 5 & 6 platoons relieved No 1 & 2 in trenches for 24 hours instruction	
27th April LAGORGUE	In billets. No 9, 10, 13 & 14 Platoons sent to trenches for 24 hours instruction	
28th April LAGORGUE	In billets. Bomb section formed under Lt SILCOCK joined Bde Grenadier Coy. Six platoons sent to trenches with Scots Guards. One major went O.C.D.	
29th April LAGORGUE	In billets. Four platoons sent to trenches for 24 hours instruction	
30th April LAGORGUE	In billets. The 4 platoons undergoing instruction were not relieved. Rations sent to the ---- and not to the trenches owing to heavy shell fire. General Trenches one man killed in trenches. Total strength 30 officers 1007 other ranks. Tighty Knight 29 Officers 973 other ranks	

146th Inf.Bde.
49th Div.

1/8th BATTN. THE WEST YORKSHIRE REGIMENT.

M A Y

1 9 1 5

Army Form C. 2118.

WAR DIARY
or
INTELLIGENCE SUMMARY.
1/9 West Yorkshires Batt.
(Erase heading not required.)

Instructions regarding War Diaries and Intelligence Summaries are contained in F.S. Regs., Part II. and the Staff Manual respectively. Title pages will be prepared in manuscript.

Hour, Date, Place	Summary of Events and Information	Remarks and references to Appendices
1st May 1915 LA GORGUE	In billets. Heavy shell fire heard in early hours of morning	
6.10 AM	Verbal instructions from Bde HQrs to stand to Arms	
10.20 AM	Orders received to resume normal conditions. Billeting party sent to BAC ST MAUR	
12.30 PM 2nd May 1915 9.1 AM LA GORGUE	Battalion inspected by Bde Cmdr. The 4 billeting returned from BINCHIN Moved to Billets at BAC ST MAUR	
10.30 AM BAC ST MAUR	Arrived BAC ST MAUR	
3rd MAY BAC ST MAUR	In billets	
4th MAY BAC ST MAUR	In billets	
5th MAY CAMERON LANE (M.21.b)	Marched from BAC ST MAUR (right MG Section). Half Batt'n took over new billets. Left half Bn relieved 6th BORDONS in Kinchen.	
	Transport parked at near ESTAIRES at 6.32	
6th MAY M.21.b	Batt'n (less C & D companies & Machine Guns) in Billets. C & D companies and MG section in Kinchen	
7th MAY M.21.b	As for 6th inst. Casualties 2 men wounded. Orders to take over new line of trenches in area of operations. Owing to postponement of operations orders cancelled. Casualties one man killed. Fighting strength 30 officers 1005 other ranks. Total strength 29 officers 960 other ranks.	

(73989) W4141—463. 400,000. 9/14. H.&J.Ltd. Forms/C. 2118/10.

WAR DIARY
or
INTELLIGENCE SUMMARY.

Army Form C. 2118.

Hour, Date, Place	Summary of Events and Information	Remarks and references to Appendices
8th May 1915 M.21.b 8:30 PM	H.Q. & half (C) Coy in billets, half A Coy & M.G. in trenches, one company in trenches (C. Coy) relieved by a coy & heavy of 6th West Yorks by daylight into reserve. The reserve company took over posts C.2 & C.3 with 2 platoons A & D coys, relieved 2 coys of "R.S. Fusiliers" in trenches	
9th May 1915 M.22.c sore S of LAVANTIE 5 AM to 6.30 AM	H.Q. took over H.Q. of 1/5/RSF / WEST RIDING IN=BDE ordered to aid Bavarian initial attack was made on right & left by other troops on 9th inst. Our artillery carried out heavy bombardment of enemies lines after which troops on right & left of our Brigade attacked the enemy. This Brigade, in accordance with orders, remained in their trenches and carried the enemy's communication trenches with fire enfilade 1/6 W.Y.R. and 1/6 W.R. There was any movement. The enemy shelled our trenches, without much effect. Total casualties killed 7. Wounded 10 two of whom died on their way to hospital.	
3.20 pm	Our artillery resumed the bombardment of hostile trenches. No further movement was made by our brigade or by the enemy. Throughout the night our men were able to repair most of the damage done from trenches during the day.	
10th May 1915 M.22.c 3:30 AM	It was reported by Art. observation officer that the enemy were concentrating in trenches to our front, but no attack was made. A few shells were fired about trenches but had no effect. The remainder of the day was exceptionally quiet. At 9 pm we were warned to be specially on the alert & prepare for any act of aggression by the enemy. This warning caused A company to stand to arms at 9.30 pm - but the coming of dawn of the next day ??? found the coy or others of them on the trenches. Lt. Pinon (wounded) no 9162 - Infantry died during day	

WAR DIARY
or
INTELLIGENCE SUMMARY.
(Erase heading not required.)

Army Form C. 2118.

Instructions regarding War Diaries and Intelligence Summaries are contained in F.S. Regs., Part II. and the Staff Manual respectively. Title pages will be prepared in manuscript.

Hour, Date, Place	Summary of Events and Information	Remarks and references to Appendices
11th May 1915 M.22.d.	Still holding trenches in M.22.b and M.22.d with A.B.&D. Coys. with 2 platoons of C. Coy in forts C2 and Q.Q.3. 2 platoons C. Coy in support. Still heavy shell fire. Casualties 1 killed 12 wounded.	
12th May 1915 M.22.d.	7th Bavarians D.Co. went out of trench smoking & within 20 yds. of our trenches. Thought our coys. had gone. Our firing when every could be on them but our 8 newly killed Germans at a few paces. To the K.O.S.B. who relieved D. Company. The two platoons of D. Company from the fort relieved D. Company during the night. The 2 platoon of C. from reserve took over forts C2 & C3. D. Company brought into reserve. Reserve company will in future carry all rations for companies in trenches as an experimental system. After casualties killed 1 wounded 1.	
13th May 1915 M.22.d.	A, B & C company in trenches. 2 platoons of fort A and D company in reserve. Very quiet throughout the day. Casualties about 9 or 1.	
14th May 1915 M.22.d. 1.G.m. 1.5 A.M.	Instructions received for artillery and rifle demonstration. Artillery demonstration commenced. All infantry of the section held by our troops opened rapid fire for two minutes after which everything quieted down. Demonstration repeated at 2 p.m. Casualties troops _____. Total strength 30 officers 992 other ranks. Fighting strength 29 officers 940 other ranks.	

(73989) W4141—463. 400,000. 9/14. H.&J.Ltd. Forms/C. 2118/10.

Army Form C. 2118.

WAR DIARY
or
INTELLIGENCE SUMMARY.
(Erase heading not required.)

Instructions regarding War Diaries and Intelligence Summaries are contained in F.S. Regs., Part II. and the Staff Manual respectively. Title pages will be prepared in manuscript.

Hour, Date, Place	Summary of Events and Information	Remarks and references to Appendices
15th May 1915 M.22.d	A, B + half C Companies in Trenches at M.29.B + M.29.D half C Coy in fosse E2 + C3, F Coy in Reserve at H.Q's. Casualties – 1 killed	
8.1 pm	Sudden must 15th Sherwood Foresters and conducted them to trenches to relieve us.	
11.50 pm	All companies aid in trenches and posts reported relief completed H. Qrs and Companies moved independently to billets at LAVANTIE The relief was carried out under heavy rifle + artillery fire without incident	
16th May 1915 LAVANTIE	Battn in billets	
17th May 1915 LAVANTIE	Battn moved from LAVANTIE to billeting area in G.31.c + region H.Q (W)B.Dio Transport parked at G.19.a	
18th May 1915 G.31.c	M.G. Sectn H.Q. with A + D Coys Two platoons D Coy has 2 platoons moved to RUE DU QUESNOY Two platoons D C2 take over Defended Posts Nos 20 + 21	
19th May 1915 RUE DU QUESNOY	In billets. Two platoons D Coy at Def Posts 20 + 21 Transport moved to	
20th May 1915 RUE DU QUESNOY	In billets. Battn isolated on account of outbreak of German measles in A, B + D Coys 1 Sgt and 11 men attached to 26th Coy R.E. Two platoons C Coy taken over dugouts in support of 6th W. Yorks at LE TROU Transport moved to RUE DU QUESNOY	
21st May 1915 RUE DU QUESNOY	In billets. Battn in isolation. Two platoons – Forts and two – Sergents TOTAL STRENGTH – Officers 30 – other ranks 991. FIGHTING STRENGTH – Officers 29 other ranks 916	

WAR DIARY
or
INTELLIGENCE SUMMARY.
(Erase heading not required.)

Army Form C. 2118.

Instructions regarding War Diaries and Intelligence Summaries are contained in F.S. Regs., Part II and the Staff Manual respectively. Title pages will be prepared in manuscript.

Hour, Date, Place	Summary of Events and Information	Remarks and references to Appendices
22nd May 1915 Bois de Dailly	Battn in billets. Inlisted. Two Platoons in fields 2 in Dugouts	
23rd May 1915 Bois de Dailly/Verquigneul	Ditto	
24th May 1915 E. M. DE QUEENCY	Ditto. Casualties — 1 killed returning from Dugout at LATROU. Base of German trench to date. One officer (Lt. O.) 26 other ranks. A + B Companies chiefly affected.	
25th May 1915 LE DE QUEENCY	In billets & fatigues as before. B + C Companies reported free from infection and allowed to proceed to fatigue parties for strengthening further trenches. No field cases reported.	
26th May 1915 LE DE QUEENCY	In billets & fatigues as before. Two platoons C Company relieve 2 of B Coy in Dugouts supporting front line trenches. No fresh cases of disease. Second billet fell in the neighbourhood of B + C Coy billets. Total strength: Officers 30 Other ranks 986.	
27th May 1915 LE DE QUEENCY	In billets + fields + alarm 130 men B Coy sent to work in trenches by day in this condition, infection than by night. + the experiment. It is the usual 70 men C Coy to work in trenches by night. 50 men D Coy to work at 1000 repairing M.G. FEUR BAIN + two others 2.1 — 2.7 May — Nil of wounded one. Wounded one.	

Army Form C. 2118.

WAR DIARY
or
INTELLIGENCE SUMMARY.
(Erase heading not required.)

Instructions regarding War Diaries and Intelligence Summaries are contained in F. S. Regs., Part II. and the Staff Manual respectively. Title pages will be prepared in manuscript.

Hour, Date, Place	Summary of Events and Information	Remarks and references to Appendices
28th May 1915 RUE QUESNOY	In Billets and post as above. All available men employed as trench digging parties in section held by 146th Bde.	
29th May RUE QUESNOY	Ditto	
30th May RUE QUESNOY	Battn declared free from infection. Ordered to relieve 1/5 West-York Regt in section 1B. Relief of trenches commenced at 8.30 p.m. completed 10.30 p.m. B, C & D Companies occupy R1, S1 & R2 respectively. A Coy holds Posts X1, B1, C1, with 2 platoons in support trenches and 2 sections attached to D Company in fire trenches. Saphead in P2 held by 1 officer & 20 men of D company. HQrs at LETROU. Trenches dry on the whole.	
31st May LE TROU RUE PETILLON	In trenches as above. A great deal of work required to improve parapets parados and traverses. A new communication started by 1/5 W.Y.Regt from LE TROU to S1 must be made safe; this will require a lot of work as will entail considerable risk to working parties being in full view of enemy trenches	

(73989) W4141—463. 400,000. 9/14. H.&J.Ltd. Forms/C. 2118/10.

146th Inf.Bde.
49th Div.

1/8th BATTN. THE WEST YORKSHIRE REGIMENT.

J U N E

1 9 1 5

Army Form C. 2118.

WAR DIARY
or
INTELLIGENCE SUMMARY.
(Erase heading not required.)

Instructions regarding War Diaries and Intelligence Summaries are contained in F.S. Regs., Part II. and the Staff Manual respectively. Title pages will be prepared in manuscript.

Hour, Date, Place	Summary of Events and Information	Remarks and references to Appendices
1st June 1915 LE TROU	In Trenches as above. Nothing of importance occurred. Good work done in improving trench line communication trench and H.Q. dugouts. At 10 a.m. offrs shelled but no damage was done.	
2nd June 1915 LE TROU	In Trenches. Trench mortar under R.A. officer set up in S.I.	
3rd June LE TROU	In Trenches. On our right are the 2nd Bn W.Y. Regt., on our left the 6th Bn W.Y. Regt. Casualties 28th May to 3rd June:- Killed 2; Died of wounds 1; Wounded 6	
4th June 1915	6/2 WY Regt. In honour of the King's birthday at 6 p.m. a few du joies were fired along the front of the 8th & 6th W.Y. Regt. The cheers somewhat followed by the national anthem and three cheers. The feu de joie came considerably earlier in the German lines, a major the man three parapets & open rapid fire but this caused no damage. The three cheers brought over a trench mortar shell which fell short before the all was quiet	

(73989) W4141—463. 400,000. 9/14. H.&J.Ltd. Forms/C. 2118/10.

WAR DIARY
or
INTELLIGENCE SUMMARY.
(Erase heading not required.)

Army Form C. 2118.

Instructions regarding War Diaries and Intelligence Summaries are contained in F.S. Regs., Part II. and the Staff Manual respectively. Title pages will be prepared in manuscript.

Hour, Date, Place	Summary of Events and Information	Remarks and references to Appendices
4th June 1915 LE TROU	In Trenches as above. Total Strength:- Officers 30; other ranks 973	
5th June 1915 LE TROU	In Trenches. Relieved in trenches by 1/5th West York. Regt. Relief commenced with one company at 7.30 p.m. to left of line. Later a night company relief commenced 8.45 p.m. completed 10.20 p.m. Returned to billets in RUE QUESNOY and RUE DU QUESNE which had been occupied by 1/5th during our tour of duty in trenches. Two Platoons A Coy remain in dugouts in support of 1/5 W.Y. Regt. Two platoons C Coy held defensive posts 20 and 21.	
6th June RUE QUESNOY	In rest billets as above. Battalion very concerned about anti-asphyxiating Gas respirators - new alteration in pattern to units.	
7th June RUE QUESNOY	In billets	

Army Form C. 2118.

WAR DIARY
or
INTELLIGENCE SUMMARY.
(Erase heading not required.)

Instructions regarding War Diaries and Intelligence Summaries are contained in F. S. Regs., Part II. and the Staff Manual respectively. Title pages will be prepared in manuscript.

Hour, Date, Place	Summary of Events and Information	Remarks and references to Appendices
8th June 1915 RUE QUESNOY	In billets. Two Platoons B relieve 2 platoon A in support of 1/5 WY Regt. Battn with HQrs at RUE QUESNOY ordered to hold the two coys billets near H.Q. as Divisional reserve. Thunderstorm during afternoon but very little rain.	
9th June 1915 RUE QUESNOY	In billets. Two platoons B Coy relieve 2 platoon C company in advanced posts 20 + 21 leaving C coy free for divisional reserve with D coy. All officers of Battn complete an attendance at lecture on Field Engineering delivered by R.E. Officer.	
10th June 1915 RUE QUESNOY	In Billets. Total Strength:- Officers 30: Other ranks 966 Casualties 4th – 10th June :- Died of wounds 1: Wounded 6	
11th June 1915 RUE QUESNOY	In Billets. Move to take over B1 and C1 relieve 1/5 W.Y. Regt A C & D Coys in trench line in order named from right to left. B coy in support and holding defended posts X1 B1 and C.1	

Army Form C. 2118.

WAR DIARY
or
INTELLIGENCE SUMMARY.
(Erase heading not required.)

Instructions regarding War Diaries and Intelligence Summaries are contained in F.S. Regs., Part II. and the Staff Manual respectively. Title pages will be prepared in manuscript.

Hour, Date, Place	Summary of Events and Information	Remarks and references to Appendices
12th June 1915 LE TROU	In trenches as above. Commenced filling in sap on left of line. Many dead in front of trenches and in sap buried. System of snipers and sniping officers organised.	
13th June 1915 LE TROU	In trenches as above. Line extended to the left as far as N.26.d.7.	
14th June 1915 LE TROU	In trenches. High explosive shell struck dugout of M.G. officer and hurt; fuse also used though dugout of O.C. right company but caused no injury to officers or men except slight wound to ear of Lt. Powys. (See exhibit 10)	
15th June 1915 LE TROU	In trenches.	
16th June 1915 LE TROU	In trenches.	

WAR DIARY or INTELLIGENCE SUMMARY.

(Erase heading not required.)

Army Form C. 2118.

Instructions regarding War Diaries and Intelligence Summaries are contained in F. S. Regs., Part II. and the Staff Manual respectively. Title pages will be prepared in manuscript.

Hour, Date, Place	Summary of Events and Information	Remarks and references to Appendices
17th June 1915 LE TROU	In trenches. Relieved from trenches by 1/5 W.Y. Regt. relief completed at 10.10 P.M. Battn. returned to billets previously occupied. Casualties 11th – 17th June :- Killed 1: Died of wounds 1: Wounded 9. Accidentally wounded 1. Other ranks 955. Total strength - officers 30.	
18th June 1915 RUEQUESNOY	In Billets. 2 Company's billets had fifteen shells fired into it during the morning, one man was slightly wounded and 2½ rifles damaged. Company moved billets after midday Post 20.	
19th June 1915 RUEQUESNOY	In billets.	
20th June 1915 RUE QUESNOY	In billets	

Army Form C. 2118.

WAR DIARY
or
INTELLIGENCE SUMMARY.
(Erase heading not required.)

Instructions regarding War Diaries and Intelligence Summaries are contained in F.S. Regs., Part II. and the Staff Manual respectively. Title pages will be prepared in manuscript.

Hour, Date, Place	Summary of Events and Information	Remarks and references to Appendices
21st June 1915 RUE QUESNOY	In billets	
22nd June 1915 RUE QUESNOY	In billets. 2nd Lieut ELKINGTON returned from hospital at HAVRE. The Battn has sent patients in having oftensed weather whenever in trenches except when holding own trenches N.W. of NEUVE CHAPELLE	
23rd June 1915 RUE QUESNOY	In billets. Commence relief of 1/5 W.Y. Regt in trenches viz. B 1 at 6 p.m. Confirmed 10.45 pm A, B, D, in trenches in order named from left to right & left. C. Co in support and supplying posts X1 B1 & C1, also 2 sections attached to left company in trenches. Total strength Officers 20 other ranks 952	
24th June 1915 LE TROU 25th June LE TROU	In trenches as above. Received instructions to hand over trenches and defensive posts to 24th Inf. Bde in order to be free to move to new trench line between QUINQUE RUE and FESTUBERT. Relief arranged to commence at 9.15 p.m. in relieving troops arrive at 10.35 p.m. Relief duly area completed 1.40 am 26th and carried out under trying conditions owing to heavy rain all day which filled the communication trenches with water reaching well above the knees in many places	
26th June 1915 LE TROU 7.30 pm	Relief of 1/5 W.Y. by 2nd Inf. Bde completed at 1.40 am. Battn marches to rest billets (G.21) 1½ miles N.W. of SAILLY-SUR-LYS. Order to move south to FESTUBERT cancelled. Move to billets ½ mile N. of DOULIEU	

Army Form C. 2118.

WAR DIARY
or
INTELLIGENCE SUMMARY.
(Erase heading not required.)

Instructions regarding War Diaries and Intelligence Summaries are contained in F. S. Regs., Part II. and the Staff Manual respectively. Title pages will be prepared in manuscript.

Hour, Date, Place	Summary of Events and Information	Remarks and references to Appendices
27th June 1915 ½ mile N. of DOULIEU	Battn in billets N. of DOULIEU. Orders received to prepare to move northwards on 28th. Heavy showers during the day	
28th June 1915 N. of DOULIEU	In billets. Absence parties under Capt WHEROKE held and northwards at 10 a.m. destination unknown. Battn moved to be prepared to move at 8 P.M. Battn moved to billets one mile South of FLETRE	
29th June 1915 1 mile S. of FLETRE	Battn marches in heavy rain to PROVEN by night with remainder of Brigade	
30th June 1915 PROVEN	Battn conveyed in motor buses to join 11th BDE in 4th Division and go into support in area recently taken over from the French on extreme left of British line two miles S.E. of ELVERDINGHE. Casualties 25th June – 1st July Killed O: field of war OR 1: Wounded OR 7. Accidentally wounded OR 1.	

(73989) W4141—463. 400,000. 9/14. H.&J.Ltd. Forms/C. 2118/10.

146th Inf.Bde.
49th Div.

1/8th BATTN. THE WEST YORKSHIRE REGIMENT.

J U L Y

1 9 1 5

Attached:

Appendix "A".

Army Form C. 2118.

WAR DIARY
or
INTELLIGENCE SUMMARY.
(Erase heading not required.)

Instructions regarding War Diaries and Intelligence Summaries are contained in F.S. Regs., Part II. and the Staff Manual respectively. Title pages will be prepared in manuscript.

Hour, Date, Place	Summary of Events and Information	Remarks and references to Appendices
1st July 1915 P.M. S.E. of ELVERDINGHE	Battn. in support position in bivouacs at CHATEAU ELVERDINGHE with one coy. in bivouacs of "H" Rede. Working parties sent to carry out R.E. work in support area by day and large parties sent for work by night on front line and communication trenches. Bathe parties - batches parts in Brigade. Total Strength Officers 30: Other ranks 943	
2nd July 1915 A.M. S.E. ELVERDINGHE	Position and work as on 1st inst.	
3rd July 1915 P.M. S.E. ELVERDINGHE	In billets & dugouts as shown. Coys. working and carrying parties sent to front line trenches. Enemy using large numbers of gas bombs and shells. Gas effects men's eyes when as tho: mostly but men were very seriously effected and were able to carry out their work allotted to them, with a few exceptions who had to sent to hospital suffering from the poisoning. This was the first experience of us in this battn. and all men behaved exceedingly well Re. damp no casualties and none losing hosh a.d. 18 NCOs + men were admitted to hospital suffering from gas poisoning.	
4th July 1915 A.M. S.E. of ELVERDINGHE	To the moves at 9 p.m. with the exception of large working parties in communication trenches, to Reserve bivouac at CHATEAU ELVERDINGHE. Working parties moving direct to ELVERLINGHE in completion of work; the last party reaching bivouac at 4 a.m. 5th inst. Total Strength Officers 30: other ranks	

Army Form C. 2118.

WAR DIARY
or
INTELLIGENCE SUMMARY.
(Erase heading not required.)

Instructions regarding War Diaries and Intelligence Summaries are contained in F.S. Regs., Part II. and the Staff Manual respectively. Title pages will be prepared in manuscript.

Hour, Date, Place	Summary of Events and Information	Remarks and references to Appendices
5th July 1915 (CHATEAU ELVERDINGHE)	In bivouacs. Complete orders and details of attack to be made on German Trenches opposite left of 11th Bde as per attached orders. The Batt'n being in reserve. Strength of Tactical war establishment strength reduced to 800.	APPX A
6th July 1915 CHATEAU ELVERDINGHE	In bivouacs. Attack successfully carried out without ulling of reserves. During night 6th-7th large working parties got to the captured Trenches and put them in a state of defence, the enemy firing very little trouble there being any little rifle fire, and shell fire not reaching the front line trenches.	
7th July 1915 CHATEAU ELVERDINGHE	In bivouacs as above. 146th Bde taken over Trenches of 12th Inf Bde. This Batt'n known to be bivouacd at CHATEAU ELVERDINGHE and CHATEAU DES TROIS TOURS and soon under orders of 146th Bde.	
8th July 1915 CHATEAU DES TROIS TOURS	In bivouacs. Working parties commenced defensive arrangements round CHATEAU DES TROIS TOURS. Batt'n in Divisional Reserve to A/Lt Col Bennett which has taken over from 4th Division 17th May. Casualties 2nd–8th July. Wounded H. Admitted to Hospital with gas poisoning 18. Total strength Officers 30 Other ranks 938.	

Army Form C. 2118.

WAR DIARY
or
INTELLIGENCE SUMMARY.
(Erase heading not required.)

Instructions regarding War Diaries and Intelligence Summaries are contained in F.S. Regs., Part II. and the Staff Manual respectively. Title pages will be prepared in manuscript.

Hour, Date, Place	Summary of Events and Information	Remarks and references to Appendices
9th, 10th, 11th, 12th July 1915 CHATEAU DES TROIS TOURS Sheet 28 G-14 D.1.1. CHATEAU DES TROIS TOURS	Batt'n in Divisional Reserve (49th W.R. Div) on ground round the Chateau.	
13th July	In bivouac as above. Batt'n was to relieve 1/7th West York Reg't on new line of trenches taken over by 146th Inf. Bde. Batt'n was to have started from bivouac a 9 P.M. but a heavy bombardment was commenced and orders were received from bivouac to the effect that orders were to remain in Divisional Reserve in case of emergency until further orders were received. An attack was being made on the left ((148th)) Brigade of the Division. At 11 P.M. the attack had been repulsed and the Artillery bombardment slackened; we then received orders to proceed with relief of 1/7 W.Y. REGT. The relief was completed and 1/7th W.Y. Reg't arrived before daylight. Lieut T.P. REAY took over charge of machine gun ~~and Lieut HAWTHORNE fought~~ *(ms)*	
14th July C.14 D.1.1. (Sheet 28)	In trenches. For the Third Time since joining the expeditionary force we have from battn of the WESTYORK REG'T together. The previous reasons being the 9th MAY when the 6th B'n. 8th B'n. 7th B'n. 5th B'n. 1st. B'n. were in the front-line side by side as named from right to left- North of NEUVE CHAPPELLE. The next reason was when the four battns Att. were heavy the 2nd & 1st & 3rd & TROY *(ms)*	

(73989) W4141—463. 400,000. 9/14. H.&J.Ltd. Forms/C. 2118/10.

WAR DIARY
or
INTELLIGENCE SUMMARY.
(Erase heading not required.)

Army Form C. 2118.

Hour, Date, Place	Summary of Events and Information	Remarks and references to Appendices
15th July 1915. C.14.D.1.1. (Sheet 20)	In Trenches A & B in front line C & D in support. WILKINSON, CLOUGH. 2/Lt Wilkinson & Rfm Clough & Mudd went on patrol in front of Trenches. He letter was shot through the chest, his cries brought heavy fire from the GERMANS round the loophole 2/Lt WILKINSON and Rfm CLOUGH carried him back to our Trenches. Before being able to pass through the barbed wire it was necessary for Rfm CLOUGH to come in and get wire cutters with which he returned. 2/Lt WILKINSON and Rfm CLOUGH were recommended for the Military Cross and D.C.M. respectively.	
16th July 1915 C.14.D.1.1. (Sheet 20)	In Trenches. Front line trenches heavily shelled by GERMANS who had established positions. Machine Gun emplacements. One of them shells killed 2/Lt C. HARTNELL. This is our first casualty amongst the officers of the Regt Battn.	
17th July 1915	C + D Companies relieved A + B in front line Trenches, A + B going into support. In Trenches	
18th July 1915 C.14.D.1.1 Sheet 20	In Trenches. At 7 P.M. we received a message from Bde. to the effect that the enemy were reported to be massing opposite the left of our division and we were warned to be in readiness; but no attack was made much to the disappointment of our men who were longing to come to closer quarters with the enemy.	
19th July 1915 C.14.D.1.1. Sheet 20	In Trenches. Our Battn relieved in Trenches by 1/7 W.Y. Regt. and we moved into Bde reserve on CANAL BANK with one company (A) in support of 1/7 W.Y. Regt.	
20th July 1915 CANAL BANK	In Bde reserve dug outs.	

Army Form C. 2118.

WAR DIARY
or
INTELLIGENCE SUMMARY.
(Erase heading not required.)

Instructions regarding War Diaries and Intelligence Summaries are contained in F. S. Regs., Part II. and the Staff Manual respectively. Title pages will be prepared in manuscript.

Hour, Date, Place	Summary of Events and Information	Remarks and references to Appendices
21st July 1915. Canal Bank	In Bde. Reserve dugouts. Issued shells filled in canal and on the banks during the day.	
22nd July Canal Bank	In Bde. Reserve as above	
23rd July Canal Bank	In Bde. Reserve as above	
24th July Canal Bank	In Bde. Reserve as above	
25th July Canal Bank	In Adv. Reserve as above. Relieved 1/7th West York. Regt in trenches. A & B in front line, C & D in support. Relief carried out without incident.	
26th July C.14.D.1.1. Sheet 28	In trenches	
27th July 1915. C.14.D.1.1. Sheet 28	In trenches	
28th July C.14.D.1.1.	In trenches as above. It has been decided to try keeping the companies in the same position throughout the six days instead of changing front line and supports after three days.	
29th July C.14.D.1.1.	In trenches	

30th July 1915
C. 14. D.I.I.

In trenches. Lieut Hon A.D. Kitson KITSON and Capt. TETLEY joined from 2/5th W.Y. Regt.
About 9.30 P.M. 2nd LIEUT WILL and No 1960 Rfm BROOKE whilst repairing the wire
were in front of our parapet heard some movement beyond our wire and then
heard a low whistle. They replied with a similar whistle and two men stood up
beyond our wire. 2/Lt WILL thereupon to them thinking they were our men,
but getting no reply, and being unarmed he pointed his finger at them
and shouted "Hands up". The men at once held up a white handkerchief
and put up their hands. 2/Lt WILL and Rfm BROOKE then went to them and
took away their arms. The two men belonged to the 238th Regt: they were
at once sent to the Bde where useful information was obtained from them.
The Divisional commander congratulated the 18th on the capture of the two prisoners
saying that they were badly required for purpose of identification.

31st July 1915
C. 14. D.I.I.

In trenches. Relieved in trenches by 1/7th W.Y. Regt. and move to dugouts west of
CHATEAU DES TROIS where the Battn becomes Divisional Reserve

APPENDIX "A".

APPENDIX A.

DISTRIBUTION OF INFANTRY.

Unit.	Position.	Remarks.
1. 1st Rifle Brigade	Left Sector.	To assault.
1st Som.L.I.	" "	To support.
1 officer and 40 men 9th Field Co.	" "	To assist in entrenching and revetting.
1 officer and 24 men 4th Cyclist Company.	" "	Grenadiers.
2. East Lancs.	Right sector.	To open rifle and machine gun fire and throw bombs when the assault takes place on FORTIN 17, and on the enemy's trenches to the East of that place.
3. 1st Hants. less one Company and machine gun section.	In Brigade support area under cover.	Reserve.
1 Company and two machine guns.	Trenches B.18 d.	Ready to move at short notice.
Two machine guns under an officer.	Entrenched on West canal bank about 60 to 80 yards south of lock B 12 d S.Y	To be able to fire up valley South of FERME 14, and on the slopes leading down from hedge East of farm, when the assault takes place.
4. Lancs Fusiliers.	Billets A 21.	Reserve. Will reconnoitre best routes on both sides of canal bank leading to fire and support trenches now held by 11th Bde.
5. 8th West Yorks.	Elverdinghe	Reserve.

W. Yorks.

APPX A

11th Infantry Brigade Copy No... 16

With reference to Operation Order No 1 of 3/7/15.

1. An issue of rum will be made to the troops, in the trenches on the night prior to the attack.

2. The G.O.C. wishes all men to have a good breakfast on the morning in question.

3. With reference to para.5 the bombing parties will carry a flag about one yard square with red and yellow quarters.

4. The following medical arrangements made by the Division are published for your information.

   (a) The advanced dressing stations will be found by No.12 Field Ambulance and will be situated in HULL'S FARM B.18 c 9.5 and LODI FARM B.24 b 2.1

   (b) One bearer subdivision will be posted at East bank of the canal in communication trench leading to bridge 6 D. Wounded will be handed over to this bearer subdivision by the Regimental stretcher bearers, who will receive stretchers from the bearer subdivision in place of the ones occupied by the wounded, and on receipt will immediately return to their Regimental Aid Posts. Seriously wounded will be carried by the stretcher squads of the bearer subdivision across bridge 6 D. and thence along the canal bank as far as bridge 6 B. at which point they will be carried direct to dressing station in HULL'S FARM.

   (c) Walking cases after being dressed at the Regimental Aid Posts are to be directed to walk down the communication trench along the East bank of the canal to No.6 pontoon bridge, which bridge they will cross and proceed to dressing station at LODI FARM.

4.7.15.

W.L. Clark
Captain.
Brigade Major, 11th Inf. Bde.

APPENDIX B

COMMUNICATIONS 11th BDE.

Telephone Stations ●
Telephone Lines shewn dotted ----
Alternatur Visual ————
Orderlies — - —

Labels on map:
- Ferme 14
- R.I.F. BRIC Somerset J.S.
- Alternative H.Q.
- F. Lane
- Bn N
- Zwaanhof
- S Zwaanhof
- 6c
- 6a
- E. Lanes
- H.A.R.
- 32 F.A.B.
- Railway
- Hulls Fm
- 14th F.A.B.
- Sarragossa
- Hauts Fm
- French Bde on left flank
- 11th Bde
- 4th Div
- French Heavy Arty

S E C R E T.

Copy No...16...

Reference map
BOESINGHE___1___
       10,000

OPERATION ORDER NO.1
by Brig-Genl C.B.PROWSE.
Comdg. 11th Infantry Bde.

1. The line of German trenches from the southern saphead C 7 c 4.4 to the point where the trenches turn North at the bend of the road C.7 c 2.8 will be assaulted ~~xxxx~~ date and hour ~~xxxx~~ will be notified later. The line of the road C 7 c 4.7 to C 7 c 2.8 will be occupied and entrenched.

2. The enemy's trenches will be bombarded for an hour, according to instructions issued to all concerned. All troops will keep well under cover during this phase.

3. The dispositions of the Infantry is shown in Appendix A.
   The assault will be delivered by the 1st Rifle Brigade supported by the 1st Somerset Light Infantry, both under the Command of Lt.Col SEYMOUR.

4 (a) Appendix B shows:-
   1. Positions of Dressing Stations and aid posts.
   2. Positions of bridges and of the R.E. for repairing the bridges.
  (b) Appendix C shows:-
   1. Positions of Headquarters of Artillery and Infantry Brigades and Battalions.
   2. Signal communications.

5. The assaulting troops will carry flags for showing the limits of their advance. These flags will be ~~about one yard~~ square ~~with yellow and red quarters.~~ RED about 18"

6. The West Lancs Field Company R.E., who are responsible for repairing the bridges, will be notified at once by telephone if any of the bridges are damaged.

7. As the phases of the bombardment and the hour for assault will be worked by time, the synchronising of all watches is of the utmost importance. Watches will be set at 11th Inf.Bde Head Quarters ~~xxxx~~ date and hour ~~xxxx~~ will be notified later. Adjutants of Artillery and Infantry will bring at least two watches each.

8. Reports to MORDACQ FARM B.17 c.d. south.

                                          W.A. Charles

                                             Captain.
                              Brigade Major,11th Inf.Bde.

3.7.15.

Copies to:-
  ✓1 & 2 Adv. 4th Div.
  ✓3 to 8 4th Div. Arty.
    9 &10 10th and 12th Bdes.   No.16 8th West Yorks. ✗
  ✓11 Rif.Brig.   17 90th Bie Français.
  ✓12 Som.L.I.   18 to 20 File.
  ✓13 East Lancs.
  ✓14 Hants.
    15 Lancs Fusrs.

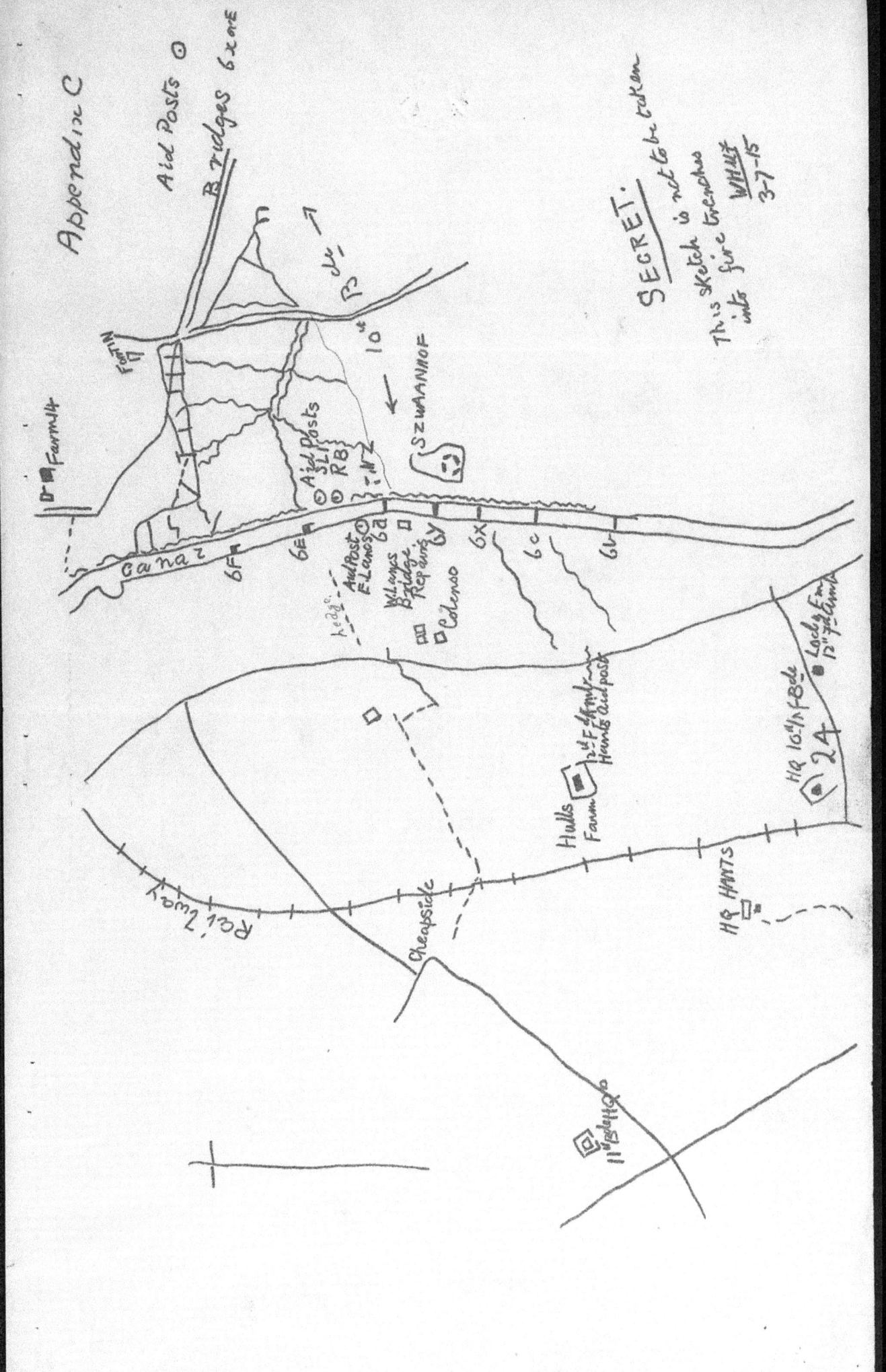

S E C R E T .　　　　　　　　　　　　　　　　Copy No....7.

　　　With reference to Operation Order No.1 dated 3rd July 1915 para. 1 : the attack will take place tomorrow, 6th July.

　　　The bombardment will commence at five am and the assault will be delivered at six am.

　　　Reference para. 7 watches will be compared at 11th Infantry Brigade Headquarters at 5-30pm today.
NOTE: The Rifle Brigade will inform Lt.COOK, 32nd Trench Howitzer Battery of the time.

　　　Acknowledge.

　　　　　　　　　　　　　　　　W.B. Charles
　　　　　　　　　　　　　　　　Captain.
　　　　　　　　　　　　Brigade Major, 11th Inf.Bde.

5.7.15.

Copies to:-

10th Bde.	1
Rif Brig	2
Som L.I.	3
East Lancs	4
Hants	5
Lancs Fusrs	6
West Yorks	7
90th French Inf.Bde	8
File	9 - 12

S E C R E T .

will	go	into	bivouac now
occupied by	R.F.	BDE	to all
ELVERDINGHE	wood	add	
units concerned			

FROM PLACE & TIME: 11th BDE 2.35 PM

SB 12PM 120 ZK
Sg. Taylor N.

Service Instructions.
ZK PRIORITY

Charges to Pay / Office Stamp
AW
4/7/15
D.55P

TO SOMEL.I. HANTS EAST LANCS R. BDE WEST YORKS

Sender's Number	Day of Month		In reply to Number	AAA
BM 267	4th			
Relief	tonight	as	follows	aaa
Right	Sector	EAST	LANCS	will
relieve	HANTS	between	9.30PM	and
11.30PM	using	bridges	6C	and
6X	aaa	The	HANTS	will
move	into	the	support	area
which	area	will	be	vacated
by	the	8th	WEST	YORKS
between	9.15PM &		9.30PM	who
will	go	into	bivouacs	at
ELVERDINGE	aaa	Left	Sector	RIFLE
BDE	L will	relieve	the	SOM.
L	1	between	11.30PM &	
1.30AM	using	bridges	6Y	&
6F	aaa	Bridge	6D	will
be	reserved for		working	parties
aaa	The	SOM.	L	1

FROM
PLACE & TIME

146th Inf.Bde.
49th Div.

1/8th BATTN. THE WEST YORKSHIRE REGIMENT.

A U G U S T

1 9 1 5

WAR DIARY

1st August 1915
TROIS TOURS
(near BRIELEN) — Batalion in Divisional Reserve: accommodated in dugouts west of the Chateau.

2nd August
TROIS TOURS — Batt'n in Divisional Reserve. The usual number of flies in this neighbourhood renders the position unhealthy.

3rd August
TROIS TOURS — Batt'n in Divisional Reserve

4th August
TROIS TOURS — Batt'n in Divisional Reserve

5th August
TROIS TOURS — Batt'n in Divisional Reserve

6th August
TROIS TOURS — Batt'n in Divisional Reserve. Move from reserve position to front line trenches in relief of 1/4th WEST YORK Regt. Relief carried out without incident after dark.

7th August — Batt'n in Trenches: C and D Companies in front line, A and B in support
Sheet 28 C.14.93
Casualties 1st – 7th August: Officers killed Nil, wounded 1, wounded 4
Total strength of units: Officers 27, Other ranks 934

WAR DIARY

7th August 1915
Strd 28 O/R C/w C 9.3.   In trenches as above

8th August
Strd 22 O/R C/w C 9.3.   In trenches as above

10th August   In trenches as above

11th August
Strd 8 O/R C/w C 9.3.   In trenches as above

12th August
Strd 8 O/R C/w C 9.3.   In trenches as above. Relieved after dark by 1/7th WESTYORK Regt
                                 and moved to Brigade Reserve on Canal Bank

13th August
CANAL BANK   Batts in Brigade Reserve ; accommodated in dugouts

14th August
CANAL BANK   Batts in Brigade Reserve. Ordered to relieve 1/6th & 1/8th WESTRIDING on left of 1/7th WESTYORK Regt
                                 Relief commenced at 2 P.M. Battns moving by communication trenches
                                 at intervals of five minutes. Relief carried out without incident (except
                                 two minor casualties. Relief of day for two fatiguing Battns by night.
                                 Casualties 7th - 14th August Officers killed Nil; (wounded) 1 other ranks killed 4 wounded 18
                                 Total Strength of Battns Officers 26 other ranks 929

WAR DIARY

15th August 1915   In trenches. A and B Companies in front line, D in support, C in reserve.
Sheet 28 C.13.D.9.3   Trenches require to be greatly improved.
                       Permission obtained to call on 105 WEST RIDING HOWITZER Batty to retaliate purposes

16th August   In trenches as above. Willed the enemy but little attempt done
Sheet 28 C.13.D.9.3   The 105th Howitzers, when called on to retaliate caused considerable
                      damage to enemy's parapets; a quantity of timber and short iron
                      was seen to be flung into the air together with bags and clothing

17th August   In trenches. Friendly and hostile artillery active. Enemy continually
Sheet 28 C.13.D.9.3   throws trench howitzer and trench mortar shells into our trenches;
                      we are unable to retaliate owing to shortage of shells. Apt trench
                      howitzer shells are of little use and a sufficient supply of
                      heavy shells is not obtainable.

18th August   In trenches as above.
Sheet 28 C.13.D.9.3

                      Casualties 15th – 18th. Officers killed Nil Wounded 2 Other ranks Killed 1 Wounded 3
                      Total Strength of Battn. Officers 25 Other Ranks 899

WAR DIARY

19th August 1915
Shot 28 O 13 D 9 3 -.   In trenches as above.

20th August
That 9 C 3 D 9 3   In Trenches. C company relieves A in front line; A moves to reserve trenches; D company relieves B in front line and B moves into support trenches. Relief carried out during afternoon by section at five minutes interval.

21st August
That 9 C 3 D 9 3   In Trenches as above.

Casualties 14th – 21st August :– Officers killed Nil; (wounded)
                                    other ranks killed   (wounded)

Total strength of Battn :– Officers   Other ranks   Horses   Vehicles
Fighting strength of Battn :– Officers   Other ranks

22nd August
Shot 28 O 13 D 9 3   In Trenches as above.

Casualties 19th – 22nd Officers :– Killed Nil Wounded Nil Other Ranks :– Killed 2 Wounded 10
Total Strength of Battn :– Officers 26 Other Ranks 887

WAR DIARY

23rd August 1915
Sheet 28 Q.1.3 D.9.3.
In trenches as above

24th August 1915
Sheet C.1.3. D.9.3
In trenches. Battn moved into Divisional Reserve in the grounds of Chateau ELVERDINGHE after being relieved in trenches by 1/5th WEST YORKSHIRE Regt. Relief commenced at 2 P.M.
Ten days in trenches with the Battn disposed in front line, supports and reserves, have not proved too long in warm weather, and seven days fatigue of preparing reliefs.

25th August 1915
ELVERDINGHE
Battn in Divisional Reserve. Officers accommodated in chateau, other ranks in tents and dug outs under trees.

26th August 1915
ELVERDINGHE
Battn in Divisional Reserve. Grassy LEDGE CHATEAU.
One Sergt wounded. CAPT. HUST.A & DUNDAS, CAPT. HODGSON, 2/Lt P. MATLEY and five men.

27th August 1915
ELVERDINGHE
Battn in Divisional Reserve as above
Casualties 23rd to 27th Officers – Killed Nil. Wounded 3
Other Ranks – Killed 1 Wounded 5
Total Strength in Officers 24 Other Ranks 899

WAR DIARY
or
INTELLIGENCE SUMMARY.
(Erase heading not required.)

Army Form C. 2118.

Hour, Date, Place	Summary of Events and Information	Remarks and references to Appendices
Aug 28th 1915 ELVERDINGHE	Batln in divisional reserve. Transfer of B.W. officers & other ranks.	Casualties 21st – 28th Officers killed - wounded OR killed - wounded
Aug 29th 1915 ELVERDINGHE	Batln in Divisional reserve.	
Aug 30th 1915 ELVERDINGHE	Relieved 1/5 West Yorkshire Regt in front line. 'A' & 'B' right front, 'B' left front, 'C' & 'D' & 'D' in support. Relief accomplished without incident.	
Aug 31st Sheet C.17.D.43.	In trenches as above. Casualties 28th to 31st: Officers: Killed - Nil Wounded - Nil OR: Killed Nil Wounded Nil Total strength = Officers 24 Other Ranks 579	

146th Inf.Bde.
49th Div.

1/8th BATTN. THE WEST YORKSHIRE REGIMENT.

SEPTEMBER

1915

WAR DIARY
or
INTELLIGENCE SUMMARY.
(Erase heading not required.)

Army Form C. 2118.

Instructions regarding War Diaries and Intelligence Summaries are contained in F.S. Regs., Part II and the Staff Manual respectively. Title pages will be prepared in manuscript.

Hour, Date, Place	Summary of Events and Information	Remarks and references to Appendices
Sept 1 C.14.c.12	In trenches	
2 C.14.c.12.	In trenches	
3 C.14.c.12.	In trenches	
4 C.14.c.12	Relieved in trenches & used as Brigade reserve on the Canal Bank	
5 CANAL BANK	In Brigade reserve	
6 CANAL BANK	In Brigade reserve	Casualties 1-7 Sept. OFFICERS Killed — OR Killed 3 OR, Wounded — OR Wounded 931 OR
7 CANAL BANK	In Brigade reserve	To the strength of Bn on 7th Sept. 20 Officers + 931 OR
8 CANAL BANK	In Brigade reserve	B.W. gone into rest camp A.16.C. was to A.1.B.
9 CANAL BANK	Relieved by 1/5 West Riding Regt. B.W. went into Bde at A.16.A	
10 A.16.A.	In rest as above	
11 A.16.A.	In rest as above	
12 A.16.A.	In rest as above	Casualties 8-15 Sept. OFFICERS Killed — OR Killed 2, Wounded — Wounded 1
13		Total strength 23 Sept. m. 15 Sept. 23 Offrs + 925 OR
14		Working parties of 50 men nightly
15 A.16.a.	In rest as above	+ 50 men by day
16		
17		
18		
19		
20	Relieved 1/4 K.O.Y.L.I. in trenches, H.Q. at C.13.C.3.2. A.D.C, B.C in front line, A Coy D centre with 1 platoon in support, C right with platoon in support, B in support.	Casualties 16-22 OFFICERS Killed — Wounded — OR Killed 1 Wounded 3
21		HB. Total strength m 22nd 24 Offrs + 912 OR
22 C.13.C.3.2		On 22nd Cpl. L. Chapman was killed by rifle fire
23	In trenches as above	

Army Form C. 2118.

WAR DIARY
or
INTELLIGENCE SUMMARY.
(Erase heading not required.)

Instructions regarding War Diaries and Intelligence Summaries are contained in F.S. Regs., Part II. and the Staff Manual respectively. Title pages will be prepared in manuscript.

Hour, Date, Place	Summary of Events and Information	Remarks and references to Appendices
Sept 24. 1915 C.13.B.3.2.	Situation	
Sept 25 C.13.C.3.2.	Night 24-25 arrangements made for a demonstration. In trenches. A demonstration by bombardment, smoke bombs, rifle & machine gun fire was had 26 enemy attacked. Enemy returned & rifle fire was returned by rapid fire.	
26 C.13.C.3.2.	Relieved by 1/5 West Yorkshire Regt & took up quarters on CANAL BANK in Brigade Reserve	wh.3
27 CANAL BANK	In Brigade Reserve as above	Casualties 23 - 29 Sept
28 CANAL BANK	In Brigade Reserve as above	OFFICERS killed Nil
		Wounded Nil
29 CANAL BANK	In Brigade Reserve as above	O.R. Killed Nil
		" Wounded 12
30 CANAL BANK	In Brigade Reserve as above	Total Strength 23rd on 29 Sept. 27 Officers & 906 O.R. WHB

146th Inf.Bde.
49th Div.

1/8th BATTN. THE WEST YORKSHIRE REGIMENT.

O C T O B E R

1 9 1 5

Army Form C. 2118.

WAR DIARY
or
INTELLIGENCE SUMMARY.
(Erase heading not required.)

1/8 West Yorkshire Rt.

Hour, Date, Place	Summary of Events and Information	Remarks and references to Appendices
Oct 1 CANAL BANK	In Brigade Reserve.	
2. CANAL BANK	Relieved 1/5 Devonshire Regt in front line trenches. HQ at C.13.B.3.3. Relief took place without incident.	
3, 8, 13, 0, 3.3.	In trenches as above	
4, C.13.B.3.3.	In trenches as above. Heavy bombardment by enemy of front line trenches on our right Batt.	
5, C.13.B.3.3.	In trenches as above.	Casualties 1-7 Oct. OFFICERS killed — Wounded — Total Strength
6, C.13.B.3.3	In trenches as above.	O.R. killed 3 26.9.15 925
7, C.13.B.3.3	In trenches as above.	Wounded 10 eff. of quarter
8, C.13.B.3.3	In trenches. Relieved by 1/5 Batt. without incident, and took up quarters on CANAL BANK.	
9, CANAL BANK	In Brigade reserve.	
10, CANAL BANK	In Brigade reserve.	
11 CANAL BANK	In Brigade reserve	
12 CANAL BANK	In Brigade reserve	
13 CANAL BANK	In Brigade reserve	Casualties 7-14 Oct
14 CANAL BANK	In Brigade reserve. Brigade moved into Divisional reserve at COPPERNAIL FARM	OFFICERS killed — Wounded —
15		OR. killed 2
16	In Divisional Reserve. Men employed in building	Wounded 11 Total Strength off 913
17	winter quarters, instruction in	
18	grenades, & practicing attack.	
19		
20		
21		
22, C.21.C.24	Batt relieved 1st KSLI in front line. HQ at C.21.C.24 Centre. Relief without incident.	
23, C.21.C.24.	In trenches as above	Casualties 14-21
24, C.21.C.24.	In trenches as above	OFFICERS killed — Wounded —
	Batt. were relieved by 1/5 B's and moved to CANAL BANK HQ one Company "X" line, 1 Coy in reserve to 1/5 B's, 2 platoons in reserve to "X" line	OR. killed — Wounded 1 Total Strength off 907

Army Form C. 2118.

WAR DIARY
or
INTELLIGENCE SUMMARY.
(Erase heading not required.)

1/8 West Yorkshire Rgt.

Hour, Date, Place	Summary of Events and Information	Remarks and references to Appendices
Oct. 25 CANAL BANK	1. Position on Right Suffolk Rgt. on Left.	
26 CANAL BANK	Proceeded up the line to the trenches.	
27 CANAL BANK	In reserve to 1st Suffolk Batt'n. Relieved 1/7th B'n.	Casualties 21-31
29 C.21.D.4.4.	Front line without incident. Two companies in support, one in reserve.	OFFICERS Killed —
		Wounded —
30 C.20.D.4.4.	NR. NC 20 D 44 Front line trenches.	O.R. Killed 4
31 C.20.D.4.4.	In front line trenches	Wounded 17
		Total Strength 876

R. M. Anderson Major
o/c

146th Inf.Bde.
49th Div.

1/8th BATTN. THE WEST YORKSHIRE REGIMENT.

N O V E M B E R

1 9 1 5

Army Form C. 2118.

WAR DIARY
or
INTELLIGENCE SUMMARY.
(Erase heading not required.)

1/8 West Yorkshire Rt.

Hour, Date, Place	Summary of Events and Information	Remarks and references to Appendices
Nov.		Casualties 1-7 Nov.
1 C2O.D.44.	In front line trenches	OFFICERS Killed —
2 C2O.D.44.	In front line trenches. Relieved by 1/6 West Yorkshire Regt & moved to position on Right Support Bank.	Wounded 1
		O.R. Killed 1
		Wounded 9
3 CANAL BANK	In right support	Total Strength 909
4 CANAL BANK	In right support	
5 CANAL BANK	In right support. Relieved 1/7 West Yorkshire in front line trenches. Having 1/6 W.Y.R. on our left and 6th Division on the night.	Casualties 8-14
		OFFICERS Killed —
6 S15.b.	In front line trenches	Wounded —
7 C21.c.4.2½	In front line trenches D21 & D22 relieving 1/6 W.Y.Rt.	O.R. Killed 3.
8 BELLE ALLIANCE	In front line trenches	Wounded 15
9 BELLEWAARDE	In front line trenches. Relieved by 1/6 W.Y.Rt. without incident.	Total Strength 886.
10 CANAL BANK	In right support	
11 CANAL BANK	In right support. Relieved 1/7 B: in front line trenches without incident	
12 C21.c.4.2½	In front line trenches. On the night two companies out Dutres were relieved by 2nd TcL Battn on own right, one in close support, one in suffort	Casualties 15-21
13 BELLE ALLIANCE	In front line	OFFICERS Killed —
14 BELLE ALLIANCE	In Trenches. Relieved by 1/6 B: West Yorks & ire Regt without incident.	Wounded —
15 BRIELEN	In Right Support	O.R. Killed 2
16 BRIELEN	In Right Support	Wounded 6
17 BRIELEN	Relieved the 1/5 B: W.Y.Rt. in front line trenches D22 with H.Q. on CANAL BANK having our Brigade on our left & 4th Battn on own right.	Total Casualties
18 FRONT BANK	In front line trenches	Strength 894
19 CANAL BANK	Relieved by 1/7 B: W.Y.Rt. & went into Div: Reserve at A.8.B. 1.5.	
20 A86.15	In Divisional Reserve	
21 A86.15	In Divisional Reserve	

Army Form C. 2118.

WAR DIARY
or
INTELLIGENCE SUMMARY.

(Erase heading not required.)

Instructions regarding War Diaries and Intelligence Summaries are contained in F. S. Regs., Part II. and the Staff Manual respectively. Title pages will be prepared in manuscript.

1/5 West Yorkshire Rgt

Hour, Date, Place	Summary of Events and Information	Remarks and references to Appendices
NOV. 1915		
22 A & B.1.5.	In Divisional Reserve	
23 A & B.1.5.	In Divisional Reserve	
24 A & B.1.5.	In Divisional Reserve. Received "gallantry cards" for two OFFICERS and nine men.	
25 A & B.1.5.	In Divisional Reserve. Inspected by Corps Commander	
26 A & B.1.5.	In Division Reserve	
27 H & B.1.5.	Took up position in Right support at ELVERDINGHE	Casualties 2 & 30 OFFICERS killed — Wounded — O.R. killed 1 Wounded + Total Strength 870
28 ELVERDINGHE	In Right Support	
29 ELVERDINGHE	Relieved 1/5 West Yorkshire Regt in front line trenches H.Q. on CANAL BANK in trenches D 21 & D 22. Being 147th Bde on left & 146th on right.	
30 CANAL BANK	In front line trenches	

B. Wimberley c/o

146th Inf.Bde.
49th Div.

1/8th BATTN. THE WEST YORKSHIRE REGIMENT.

D E C E M B E R

1 9 1 5

Army Form C. 2118.

1/8 WEST YORKSHIRE REGT

WAR DIARY
or
INTELLIGENCE SUMMARY.
(Erase heading not required.)

Instructions regarding War Diaries and Intelligence Summaries are contained in F.S. Regs., Part II. and the Staff Manual respectively. Title pages will be prepared in manuscript.

Hour, Date, Place	Summary of Events and Information	Remarks and references to Appendices
Dec 1914/15		
1 CANAL BANK	In front line trenches D11 to D22	
2 CANAL BANK	In front line trenches	
3 CANAL BANK	In front line trenches. Relieved by 1/6 West Yorkshire Regt. & went to Right support position at ELVERDINGHE	Casualties 1st – 7th
4 ELVERDINGHE		Officers killed – 1
5 ELVERDINGHE	Relieved the 1/5 front line trenches T, having on our right 4th & K.R.R.	Wounded – 1
6 B20 D44	1/6 on our left. H.Q. at B20 D44.	O.R. Killed – 1
	In front line trenches	Wounded – 8
7 B20 D44	In front line trenches	
7/8 B20 D44	In front line trenches	Total Strength 851
9 B20 D44	In front line trenches. Relieved by 1/6 West Yorkshire Regt. & went to Right Suffolk	
10 ELVERDINGHE	In right Suffolk position at ELVERDINGHE	
11 ELVERDINGHE	In right Suffolk. Relieved 1/7 West Yorkshire Regt. in D21 D22	Casualties 8th – 14th
12 CANAL BANK	In front line trenches	Officers Killed – 1
13 CANAL BANK	Relieved by 1/5 West Yorkshire Regt. and moved to Divisional Rest at A8 B 6.15	Wounded – 1
14 A8 B 6.15	Divisional Rest	O.R. Killed – 3
15 A8 B 6.15	In Divisional Rest	Wounded – 9
16 A8 B 6.15	In Divisional Rest	
17 A8 B 6	In Divisional Rest	Total Strength 819
18 A8 B 6	In Divisional Rest	

Army Form C. 2118.

WAR DIARY
or
INTELLIGENCE SUMMARY.
(Erase heading not required.)

1/8 WEST YORKSHIRE Regt

Hour, Date, Place	Summary of Events and Information	Remarks and references to Appendices
Dec 19th A&G 1.5	In Divisional Reserve. Enemy made gas attack and Bn moved to ELVERDINGHE & went into trenches, returning to camp in the evening	Casualties 15th – 21st Officers killed — Wounded — O.R. Killed — Wounded 1 Total Strength 834
20th A&G 1.5	In Divisional Reserve	
21st A&G 1.6	In Divisional Reserve. Relieved 1/6 Bn in front line trench section T1, trench section D19 & D20 having 2nd Yorks on our right and 1/7 Bn on her left.	
22nd B.20 d.4.4. 23rd B.29 d.4.4.	In front line trenches	
	In front line trenches. Relieved by 1/5 Bn & moved to next section on left taking over D21 & D22 from 1/7th Bn & having 1/5 Bn on own right and the 147? Inf Bde on own left.	
24th BANAL BANK	In front line trenches	
25 CANAL BANK	In front line trenches	
26th CANAL BANK	In front line trenches	
27 CANAL BANK	In front line trenches. Relieved by 1/5 Bn & moved to ELVERDINGHE & took up position as Right Support Bn.	

Army Form C. 2118.

WAR DIARY
or
INTELLIGENCE SUMMARY.
(Erase heading not required.)

1/8 WEST YORKSHIRE REGT

Hour, Date, Place	Summary of Events and Information	Remarks and references to Appendices
Dec 28th ELVERDINGHE	In position on Right Suffolk Batt'n	Casualties 22nd – 31st
29th ELVERDINGHE	Moved to CAMP A30 on way to rest.	Officers killed —
30th CAMP A30	Moved to CAMP & L.3. Shed 27.	Wounded —
31st CAMP L.3.	Moved to billets in HOUTKIRQUE	O.R. killed 1
		Wounded 2
		Total Strength 819

Y Mayunder
Lt Col

Army Form C. 2118.

1/5 West Yorkshire Regt

WAR DIARY
or
INTELLIGENCE SUMMARY.
(Erase heading not required.)

Instructions regarding War Diaries and Intelligence Summaries are contained in F. S. Regs., Part II. and the Staff Manual respectively. Title pages will be prepared in manuscript.

Hour, Date, Place	Summary of Events and Information	Remarks and references to Appendices
Jan, 1916		
1st HOUTKERQUE	The Brigade moved by march route to WORMHOUDT	
2nd WORMHOUDT	} In CORPS RESERVE	Casualties 1st to 7th Nil
3rd WORMHOUDT		Total Strength of Battn 809.
4th WORMHOUDT		
5th WORMHOUDT		
6th WORMHOUDT	Training continued in squad drill	
7th WORMHOUDT		
8th WORMHOUDT	} In CORPS RESERVE	
9th WORMHOUDT		
10th WORMHOUDT		

Army Form C. 2118.

WAR DIARY
or
INTELLIGENCE SUMMARY.
(Erase heading not required.)

1/8 West Yorkshire Regt.

Instructions regarding War Diaries and Intelligence Summaries are contained in F.S. Regs., Part II. and the Staff Manual respectively. Title pages will be prepared in manuscript.

Hour, Date, Place	Summary of Events and Information	Remarks and references to Appendices
Jan 11th Wormhoudt	} In CORPS RESERVE	Casualties 8th – 14th Officers killed NIL " Wounded NIL O.R. Killed NIL " Wounded NIL Total Strength 819
12th Wormhoudt		
13th Wormhoudt		
14th Wormhoudt		
15th Wormhoudt	Brigade proceeded by march route towards CALAIS. Bn was billeted for the night in MILLAM	
16th Millam	Brigade proceeded by march route towards CALAIS. Bn was billeted for the night near ZUTKERQUE	
17th Zutkerque	Brigade proceeded to hut camp at CALAIS & proceeded to train in Corps Reserve	
18th Calais	In Corps Reserve	Casualties 15th – 21st OFFICERS Killed NIL " Wounded NIL O.R. Killed NIL O.R. Wounded NIL Total Strength 790
19th Calais	" "	
20th Calais	" "	
21st Calais	" "	
22nd Calais	" "	
23rd Calais	" "	
24th Calais	" "	
25th Calais	" "	
26th Calais	" "	
27th Calais	" "	

Army Form C. 2118.

WAR DIARY
or
INTELLIGENCE SUMMARY.

(Erase heading not required.)

1/8 WEST YORKSHIRE REGT

Instructions regarding War Diaries and Intelligence Summaries are contained in F.S. Regs., Part II and the Staff Manual respectively. Title pages will be prepared in manuscript.

Hour, Date, Place	Summary of Events and Information	Remarks and references to Appendices
Jan 28 CALAIS	In CORPS RESERVE	Casualties 22nd – 31st OFFICERS Killed } Nil " Wounded } OR. Killed } " Wounded } Total Strength 979
29 CALAIS	"	
30 CALAIS	"	WNG vice de Mont 6th W Yorks for O.C. 1/8 W Yorks
31 CALAIS	"	

(73989) W4141—463. 400,000. 9/14. H.&J.Ltd. Forms/C. 2118/10.

Army Form C. 2118.

WAR DIARY
or
INTELLIGENCE SUMMARY.
(Erase heading not required.)

1/8= 18ᵗʰ WEST YORKSHIRE REGᵀ

Hour, Date, Place	Summary of Events and Information	Remarks and references to Appendices
Feb 1 CALAIS	The Brigade moved to the neighbourhood of AMIENS by train and march route. 1/8 WEST YORKSHIRE Rᵗ billeted at FOURDRINOY	Casualties Feb 1ˢᵗ to 7ᵗʰ NIL
2 FOURDRINOY	In CORPS RESERVE	
3 FOURDRINOY	" " "	
4 FOURDRINOY	" " "	
5 FOURDRINOY	" " "	STRENGTH of Battⁿ 764
6 BREILLY	Battⁿ moved into other billets at BREILLY	
7 BREILLY	In CORPS RESERVE	
8 BREILLY	" " "	
9 BREILLY	" " "	
10 MOLLIENS-AU-BOIS	Brigade moved by march route towards ALBERT. Battⁿ billeted for the night at MOLLIENS-AU-BOIS	Casualties Feb 8ᵗʰ to 14ᵗʰ O.R. wounded 3
11 BOUZINCOURT	Brigade moved by march route to BOUZINCOURT & billeted there for the night.	
12 Front line Trenches	Battⁿ relieved 2 Companies of 16ᵗʰ Bᵗ LANCASHIRE FUSILIERS in front line trenches on NORTH & EASTERN Edge of THIEPVAL WOOD with R ANCRE on left flank. Bᵗ H.Q. at GORDON CASTLE in THIEPVAL WOOD. Troops on right 1/6ᵉ WEST YORKS, on left 36ᵉ Division. Brigade H.Q. at MARTINSART.	STRENGTH of Battⁿ 765.

Army Form C. 2118.

WAR DIARY
or
INTELLIGENCE SUMMARY.
(Erase heading not required.)

1/8 Bn WEST YORKSHIRE REGT

Hour, Date, Place	Summary of Events and Information	Remarks and references to Appendices
FEB. 13TH IN TRENCHES	In front line trenches THIEPVAL WOOD.	
14TH "	" " " " "	Casualties Feb 15th - 21st
15TH "	" " " " "	O.R. killed 2
16TH "	" " " " "	
17TH "	" " " " "	STRENGTH of Battalion
18TH "	" " " " "	463
19TH "	" " " " "	
20TH "	" " " " "	
	Bn relieved by 1/5 Bn WEST YORKS. On relief 1/8th Bn WEST YORKS. On relief Bn H.Q. with C + D Coys & Battn Grenadiers moved into Support at AUTHUILLE. A Coy remained in Close Support to 1/5th WEST YORKS at GORDON CASTLE + B Coy in Close Support to 1/5 WEST YORKS at JOHNSTONE'S POST.	
21ST IN SUPPORT AUTHUILLE, ETC	On Support at AUTHUILLE, GORDON CASTLE, + JOHNSTONE'S POST	Casualties Feb 22nd - 29th O.R. wounded 4
22nd "	" " " "	
23rd "	" " " "	
24th "	Owing to heavy snow storm weather the Batto was called on to relieve the 1/5 Bn WEST YORKS. Relief completed without incident.	STRENGTH of Battalion 466
25TH IN TRENCHES	In front line trenches THIEPVAL WOOD	
26TH "	" " " " "	
27TH "	" " " " "	
28TH "	" " " " "	

WAR DIARY
or
INTELLIGENCE SUMMARY.

(Erase heading not required.)

Army Form C. 2118.

1/8ᵗʰ Bᵗ WEST YORKSHIRE REGᵗ

Hour, Date, Place	Summary of Events and Information	Remarks and references to Appendices
FEB. 29ᵗʰ IN TRENCHES	Battⁿ relieved by 1/5ᵗʰ Bᵗ West Yorks Regᵗ. On relief Battⁿ moved into Brigade Reserve at MARTINSART	

M. H. Hutley
2nd Lt A/Adjt
for O.C. 1/8ᵗʰ Bᵗ West Yorks Regᵗ

March 1916.
Vol 7 pp 1-8
Army Form C. 2118.

WAR DIARY
or
INTELLIGENCE SUMMARY.
(Erase heading not required.)

1/8 Bn WEST YORKSHIRE REGT

Hour, Date, Place	Summary of Events and Information	Remarks and references to Appendices
MARCH 1ST		CASUALTIES MARCH 1ST-7TH
MARTINSART	In Brigade Reserve	NIL
2ND "	"	
3RD "	Bn moved to VARENNES into CORPS RESERVE	STRENGTH OF BATTALION
4TH VARENNES	In Corps Reserve	804
5TH "	"	
6TH "	BRIGADE H.Q. moved to HARPONVILLE	
7TH "	"	
8TH "	"	Employed on Railway work
9TH "	"	
10TH "	do	
11TH "	do	
12TH "		
15TH "	Moved to BEAUCOURT remaining in Corps Reserve	No casualties during the month
16TH BEAUCOURT	In Corps Reserve	Strength of Bn
26TH "		at end of March
27TH "	Moved to BAVELINCOURT remaining in Corps Reserve	OR 843
28TH "		Officers 32
16TH-31ST BAVELINCOURT	In Corps Reserve	

14b/49

1/8 W York Regt

Vol 8

April 1916

Army Form C. 2118.

1/8 West Yorkshire Regt

WAR DIARY
or
INTELLIGENCE SUMMARY.
(Erase heading not required.)

Hour, Date, Place	Summary of Events and Information	Remarks and references to Appendices
April 1916		
1 BAVELINCOURT	In Corps Reserve	
2 do	do do	
3. do	do do	
4 do	do do	
5 do	do do	
6 do	do do	
7 BAVELINCOURT	Moved to BEAUVURT	
8 ESBART	H.Q. at ESBART	
9 VIGNACOURT	Moved to VIGNACOURT in G.H.Q reserve	
10 VIGNACOURT		
11"		
H"	Remained in G.H.Q reserve	Casualties during month
16 VIGNACOURT		Officers killed NIL
		Wounded NIL
	Provided a	O.R. Killed NIL
	working party	Wounded NIL
	of 430 O.R.	Strength at end of April
30"	who were spread	999
	about the country	

Army Form C. 2118.

WAR DIARY
or
INTELLIGENCE SUMMARY.
(Erase heading not required.)

H.q West Yorkshire Regt

Hour, Date, Place	Summary of Events and Information	Remarks and references to Appendices
April 1916		
1 BARLEUCOURT	In CORPS RESERVE	
2 do	do do	
3 do	do do	
4 do	do do	
5 do	do do	
6 do	do do	
7 BARLEUCOURT	Moved to BEAUCOURT H.Q. at ESBART	
8 ESBART	Moved to VIGNACOURT in G.H.Q reserve	
9 VIGNACOURT		
10 VIGNACOURT		
11th	Remained in G.H.Q reserve sending out	Casualties during April
to	working parties 2 Offs & 30 O.R. to	NIL
30th	various villages.	Strength at end of month
VIGNACOURT		999

146/49

WAR DIARY
or
INTELLIGENCE SUMMARY.
(Erase heading not required.)

Army Form C. 2118.

May 1916.

1/8 West Yorkshire Regt.

Hour, Date, Place	Summary of Events and Information	Remarks and references to Appendices
VIGNACOURT May 1st – 31st	During this month the Batt'n remained in G.H.Q. reserve. Training in various forms was carried out & certain working parties were found.	Casualties during May OFFICERS NIL O.R. NIL Strength at end of May. Officers 41 O.R. 884 W H Doyle Lt Col Comdg 1/8 W Yorks
May 31.	The Batt'n moved to HERISSART	

146th Brigade.

49th Division.

1/8th BATTALION

WEST YORKSHIRE REGIMENT

JUNE 1916

June 1916. 146/49

Army Form C. 2118.

1/8 West Yorkshire Regt

WAR DIARY
or
INTELLIGENCE SUMMARY.
(Erase heading not required.)

Hour, Date, Place	Summary of Events and Information	Remarks and references to Appendices
June 1st HERISSART	The Battalion under the Orders of the 147th Inf Bde moved to a position in reserve to the 31st Division in AVELUY WOOD	
June 2nd to June 16th AVELUY WOOD	The Battn remained in reserve, furnishing working-parties by day and night of 250 men	2nd Lieut SISSONS & Ryn. DALTON killed & slightly & severely wounded in Avebery & O.R. wounded. Lt Gazette 27 June 3rd R.C.H. ALEXANDER gets a D.S.O.
June 17th to June 22nd AVELUY WOOD	do.	
June 22nd June 23 HERISSART	Moved to HERISSART Bde H.Q. at HERISSART Remainder of Bttn at PUCHEVILLERS	Casualties for Month OFFICERS Killed Wounded O.R. Killed Wounded
June 24 HERISSART	Draft of two officers	
June 25 HERISSART		
June 26 to June 28 HERISSART	Moved to VARENNES	Total Strength at end of month Officers 44 O.R. 1007
June 30 VARENNES	Moved to AVELUY WOOD	10 C, Adjnt

146th Inf. Bde.
49th Div.

WAR DIARY

1/8th BATTN. THE WEST YORKSHIRE REGIMENT.

J U L Y

1 9 1 6

Army Form C. 2118.

WAR DIARY
or
INTELLIGENCE SUMMARY.
(Erase heading not required.)

Instructions regarding War Diaries and Intelligence Summaries are contained in F.S. Regs., Part II. and the Staff Manual respectively. Title pages will be prepared in manuscript.

1/8 West Yorkshire Regt

Hour, Date, Place	Summary of Events and Information	Remarks and references to Appendices
JULY		Vol XI
1 THIEPVAL WOOD	Moved into THIEPVAL WOOD in immediate support to the 36th Div. Heavy fighting ensued 2/Bn the Battalion was not called on to go over the parapet. Had heavy casualties. Fighting continued during the 2nd but in the evening we moved to AVELUY WOOD.	Casualties during July
2 " "		OFFICERS
3 AVELUY WOOD	Moved in the evening to MARTINSART WOOD	Killed 2
4 MARTINSART WOOD		Wounded 12
5 } do.	Remained in Divisional Reserve	Missing 1
6 }		Gassed 1
7 } do.	Took over front line from 10th Cheshire Regt, having our HQ at Wood Post with 4th Div on right to 1/6 on left	O.R.
8 }		Killed 56
9 }		Wounded 297
10 } WOOD POST		Missing 13
11 }		Gassed 3
12 } do.	Took part in demonstrations connected with other operations	
13 }		Strength at end of month
14 }	Relieved 1/6 in LEIPZIG SALIENT	Officers 31 O.R. 705
15 } do.		unstrength
16 } LEIPZIG		
17 } do.	Enemy made heavy bombing attack but were repulsed	
18 }	Were relieved by 1/5 — went to AUTHUILLE BLUFF	
19 } HY BLUFF	Relieved 1/5 in Salient, we made an attack and took two trenches from the Guards Fusilier Regt	
20 LEIPZIG	Were relieved by 4th Y&L — moved to FORCEVILLE	
21 & 22	Remained in Corps Reserve	
23rd	Went to BOUZINCOURT in Corps Reserve	
24th BOUZINCOURT		
25 BOUZINCOURT	Moved back to FORCEVILLE	
26 }		
27 } FORCEVILLE		
28 }		
29		
30		
31 County	Relieved 1/5 at QUARRY Post — Took over a portion of front line having HQ on left of 48 Div on right	

146th Brigade
49th Division.
~~666~~----------

1/6th BATTALION

WEST YORKSHIRE REGIMENT

AUGUST 1 9 1 6

August 1916
1/8 West Yorkshire Regt.

12.C.
2 sheets

Vol 12

WAR DIARY
or
INTELLIGENCE SUMMARY.
(Erase heading not required.)

Army Form C. 2118.

Hour, Date, Place	Summary of Events and Information	Remarks and references to Appendices
Aug 1 Quarry Post to 5th 6th	Battalion holding front line trenches from (1st German line inclusive) ACROSS HOPE TRENCH - to NAB - to VIII AVENUE having two companies attached from 1/5 & 1/7 alternately, 48th Div & 12th Div alternately on our right.	
Gloucester Post 15	H.Q. only moved (to GLOUCESTER POST)	
Gloucester Post 16 Martinsart Wood 17 Martinsart Wood 18 Lealvillers	The Battalion was relieved by the 1/7 Warwickshire Regt & moved to MARTINSART WOOD. During the above tour of duty we took part - chiefly in minor demonstrations - in nine operations. On Aug 12th when we attacked we had almost attained our objective when we were stopped owing to the mid moon night exposing us however advanced our bombing block some thirty yards.	
	Moved to LEALVILLERS	
18th to 26th	Remained at Lealvillers training & organising.	

Army Form C. 2118.

WAR DIARY
or
INTELLIGENCE SUMMARY.
(Erase heading not required.)

1/5 West Yorkshire Reg

Hour, Date, Place	Summary of Events and Information	Remarks and references to Appendices
Aug. 27. HEDAUVILLE	The Battn relieved the Loyal North Lancashires at GORDON CASTLE leaving the 1/5 Bn on its right and the 6th Division on its left, relieving for dinner.	Casualties during month OFFICERS Killed 2 Wounded 1 Missing — O.R. Killed 26 Wounded 67 Missing 3
28 GORDON CASTLE	Remained in front line.	
29 GORDON CASTLE	Were relieved by 147th Bde and moved to HEDAUVILLE.	Strength at end of month. Officers 39 O.R. 608
30 HEDAUVILLE	In billets & huts in HEDAUVILLE.	
31 HEDAUVILLE	do.	

146th. INFANTRY BRIGADE
49th. DIVISION

1/8th. WEST YORKSHIRE REGT.

SEPTEMBER 1916.

September 1916

Vol 13

1/8 West Yorkshire Rgt.

WAR DIARY
or
INTELLIGENCE SUMMARY.
(Erase heading not required.)

Army Form C. 2118.

Instructions regarding War Diaries and Intelligence Summaries are contained in F.S. Regs., Part II. and the Staff Manual respectively. Title pages will be prepared in manuscript.

Hour, Date, Place	Summary of Events and Information	Remarks and references to Appendices
SEPT.	The Battn. was in billets in HEDAUVILLE	
1 HEDAUVILLE	Moved at 4 P.M. to AVELUY WOOD	
2 do		
3 AVELUY	Moved into parados in front of British line getting into position about 4.30 A.M. At 6.10 we attacked the enemy but were unable to hold and consolidate. Casualties 4 officers 294 O.R.	Casualties during month
4 FOREEVILLE	Were relieved and moved to FOREEVILLE. Company's Battalion Training at FOREEVILLE. Continued training. On 13th received notification that the Brigade had been chosen to operate as a flying column with the Cavalry in the case of the enemy's line being broken. There was however cancelled on the 14th. 15th & 16th were good days for rumours a big advance was reported. On the 16th the Battalion branched its march for the reinforcements.	Officers killed 1
5,6,7,8,9,10,11,12,13,14,15,16,17 FOREEVILLE		Wounded 5
		Missing 5
		O.R. killed 64
		Wounded 238
		Missing 81
18th Foreeville 19 Hedauville 20 Hedauville	The Battalion moved to HEDAUVILLE into Bivouacs	
	Relieved 1/4 K.O.Y.L.I. in front line 114 at Belfast City	Strength at end of month. 47 Officers 746 O.R.
27th BELFAST CITY 29 MAILLY MAILLET 30 RAINNEVAL	Were relieved by 2nd L.R. and moved to MAILLY MAILLET Moved to RAINNEVAL H. HALLDY	300 SRB 130

October 1916.

1/8 W. York Regt

Army Form C. 2118.

WAR DIARY
or
INTELLIGENCE SUMMARY
(Erase heading not required.)

1/8 West Yorkshire Rgt
Vol 14

Place	Date	Hour	Summary of Events and Information	Remarks and references to Appendices
HALLOY	Oct 1		The Battalion moved into HALLOY and continued company and battalion training, musketry and other work continuing until 11th.	
HUMBERCOURT	11		The Battalion moved into huts in HUMBERCAMP and remained there the 18th continuing training and practising the attack	
HUMBERCAMP	18		The Batt'n moved into Brigade Reserve in BIENVILLERS, having one company forward on the right, and three platoons in dugouts on VIENNA ROAD forming support and remained there until the 24th.	
BIENVILLERS	24		The Battalion moved into the front line, having the 147th Bde on the right and the 1/5th Bn. on the left, relieving the 1/7. The line was long and a considerable distance from the enemy.	
			The Battalion remained in this position until the end of the month	
			Casualties during month Officers killed Nil, wounded Nil, missing Nil.	
			O.R. " Nil, " 2, " = end of Rances	
			Strength at end of October, 868.	

W. H. Grant Lt Col

November 1916
Vol 15
1/8 Bedfordshire Rgt
15 C

WAR DIARY
or
INTELLIGENCE SUMMARY.
(Erase heading not required.)

Army Form C. 2118.

Place	Date	Hour	Summary of Events and Information	Remarks and references to Appendices
	Nov.			
FONQUEVILLERS	1		In front line trenches with 1/6 W.Y.R. on left and 1/7 W.Y.R. on right. A quiet day.	
do	2		Relieved by 1/7 W.Y.R. without incident, and moved into the billets at ST AMAND	
ST AMAND	3		Interior economy, improvement of quarters & a working party of 100 men at HÉNU	
do	4		"D" Co. no a unit took over work at ST AMAND.	
"	5		Continued training and work on camp	
"	6		do	
"	7		do	
"	8		do	
FONQUEVILLERS	9		Moved into front line trenches. HQ at FONQUEVILLERS, three coys in front line, D in support. 1/7 Brigade on right, 1/6 W.Y.R. on left. In front line trenches.	
"	10		do	
"	11		do	
"	12		do	
"	13		do	
"	14		Successful attack took place well to our right	
BIENVILLERS	15		Were relieved by 1/7 W.Y.R. & moved into billets at BIENVILLERS. Remained in support. No 2 coys working.	
	16		do	

Army Form C. 2118.

WAR DIARY
or
INTELLIGENCE SUMMARY.
(Erase heading not required.)

Instructions regarding War Diaries and Intelligence Summaries are contained in F.S. Regs., Part II. and the Staff Manual respectively. Title pages will be prepared in manuscript.

1/8 Devonshire Regt

Place	Date	Hour	Summary of Events and Information	Remarks and references to Appendices
BIENVILLERS	Nov 17		Remained in Souffel in BIENVILLERS providing large working parties.	
	18		do. do. do.	
	19		do. do. do.	
FONCQUEVILLERS	20		Relieved 1/5 Devons from trenches. Activities on night of 20/21 Place [?] on left.	
	21		As for last time	
	22		do.	
	23		do.	Casualties November
	24		do.	Officers NIL
	25		do.	O.R. killed 3 Wounded 13
SOUASTRE	26		Was relieved by 1/5 and moved to SOUASTRE. No one killed, numbers found in quiet. Strength at end of November
	27		Rested on arrival, cleaned up, getting into dry & refitting clothes &c	Officers 37
	28		do	O.R. 859
	29		do	
	30		do	

W.R. [?] Capt & Adjt

146/49.

Vol 16

16 C
3 sheets

SECRET.

WAR DIARY.

OF

1/8th Batt. West Yorks Regt

FOR

December. 1916.

Army Form C. 2118.

WAR DIARY
or
INTELLIGENCE SUMMARY.
(Erase heading not required.)

Instructions regarding War Diaries and Intelligence Summaries are contained in F. S. Regs., Part II. and the Staff Manual respectively. Title pages will be prepared in manuscript.

Place	Date 1916	Hour	Summary of Events and Information	Remarks and references to Appendices
SOUASTRE	Dec. 1st		In billets.	
—	2nd		The Battalion relieved the 1/7th West Yorkshire Regt in trenches near FONQUEVILLERS	
FONQUEVILLERS	3rd		In trenches.	
—	4th		In trenches.	
—	5th		The Battalion was relieved in trenches by the 1/5th LINCOLNSHIRE REGT & proceeded by march route to PAS via BIENVILLERS, SOUASTRE & HENU.	
PAS	6th		The Battalion proceeded by march route to LE SOUICH via MONDICOURT, LUCHEUX & went into billets there.	
LE SOUICH	7th to 31st		In billets. The Battalion carried out training.	

C.R. ?order ?t. Col.
1/8 West Yorks.

146/49
Vol 17

17C
G/UM

S E C R E T

W A R D I A R Y.

OF

18th Batt. West Yorks Regt

F O R

January 1917.

SECRET.

WAR DIARY

OF

FOR

1917.

Army Form C. 2118.

1/8 West Yorkshire R[?]

WAR DIARY
or
INTELLIGENCE SUMMARY.
(Erase heading not required.)

Place	Date	Hour	Summary of Events and Information	Remarks and references to Appendices
Le Souich	Jan 1-6		Battalion remained in billets and carried on with Company training and musketry on the miniature and open ranges. On the 2nd and 4th Jan. working parties of 4 officers and 200 men were provided for work in Lucheux Wood, chiefly consisting of making hurdles and fascines.	
"	5		2nd Lt. Lennox returned from Lewis Gun School Mondicourt	
"	6		2nd Lt. Mortimer returned from Divisional School. Grenas	
"	7		The Battalion left Le Souich by route march for Bailleulmont, passing through Brevillers, Lucheux, Humbercourt, Coullemont, Coutrelle Lahenliere, and Lacauchie a distance of 15 miles. The march was completed without any men falling out. Marching out strength 23 officers and 850 other ranks.	
Bailleulmont	8		2nd Lt Jeffrey and 2nd Lt. Baker proceeded to Divisional School Grenas	
"	8-10		Battalion in [?] Divisional reserve at Bailleulmont carrying out Company and Field training	
"	9		A party of 50 men under Corpl Kemp proceeded to Bavincourt for	

Army Form C. 2118.

1/8 Bedfordshire W

WAR DIARY
or
INTELLIGENCE SUMMARY.
(Erase heading not required.)

Place	Date	Hour	Summary of Events and Information	Remarks and references to Appendices
BAILLEULMONT	9		hut building	
"	10		A party of 10 men proceeded to Humbercamp for hut building	
"	11		The Battalion left Bailleulmont to relieve the 1/7 West Yorkshire Regt in the trenches south of Bellacourt, proceeding via Bailleulval, Basseux and Bellacourt	
TRENCHES	12		In the trenches. Patrols went out each night. Wiring was done and the trenches cleared of mud and ruts made as far as possible	
"	13-14		do	
"	15		The Battalion was relieved by the 1/7 West Yorkshire Regt and proceeded to Brigade Reserve in Bailleulval	
BAILLEULVAL	16		The Battalion bathed and refitted. At night a working party of 6 officers and 250 men was provided to work on the communication trenches in the Brigade area	
"	17-18		Working parties provided as for the 16th	
"	18		Lieut Silcock took up his duties as O.C. P.B. Company at the XVIII Corps H.Q.	

Army Form C. 2118.

WAR DIARY
or
INTELLIGENCE SUMMARY.
(Erase heading not required.)

1/8 West Yorkshire Rgt.

Hour, Date, Place		Summary of Events and Information	Remarks and references to Appendices
	1917		
BAILLEUVAL TRENCHES	Jan 19	The battalion left BAILLEUVAL and relieved the 1/7 West Yorkshire Regt in the trenches south of BELLACOURT	
"	20/22	Battalion in trenches. Patrols were sent every night and a considerable amount of work was done in clearing and repairing trenches, and hutting out wire. Enemy quiet with exception of slight shelling and sniping.	
"	23	The Battalion was relieved by 1/7 West Yorkshire Regt, and proceeded to Divisional Reserve at BAILLEUMONT	
BAILLEUMONT	24-26	Battalion carried out Company and Stokes training	
"	25	The organization of Companies was altered from this date, platoons being divided as follows:– No 1 Section, snipers No 2 Section Bombers No 3 Section, Lewis Gunners, No 4 Section Rifle Grenadiers.	

Army Form C. 2118.

WAR DIARY
or
INTELLIGENCE SUMMARY.
(Erase heading not required.)

1/8 West Yorkshire Regt

Hour, Date, Place		Summary of Events and Information	Remarks and references to Appendices
BAILLEULMONT	1917 Jan 26	No 3 Platoon under 2nd Lt Turner proceeded to Brigade School for an eight day course	
"	27	The battalion left Bailleulmont and relieved the 1/7 West Yorkshire Regt in the trenches south of Bellacourt	
TRENCHES	28/30	Battalion in the trenches. Patrols were out every night. Work on the trenches was carried out, but hindered to some extent by hard frost. A considerable amount of wire was put out. Enemy quiet with the exception of the night of the 29/30 when there was considerable trench mortar activity and slight shelling	
BAILLEULVAL	31	The battalion was relieved by the 1/7 West Yorkshire Regt and proceeded to Brigade reserve at Bailleulval. Strength 27 officers and 728 other ranks. Casualties for month - 11 other ranks, none killed	W.H. Gallof Lt Col for O.C. 1/8 W.Y. pl.

SECRET.

WAR DIARY.

OF

1/8th Batt West York Regt

FOR

February 1917.

WAR DIARY or INTELLIGENCE SUMMARY.

Army Form C. 2118.

(Erase heading not required.)

1/5 West Yorkshire Rgt

Hour, Date, Place	Summary of Events and Information	Remarks and references to Appendices
BAILLEULVAL Feb 1st	The Battalion was in billets training & finding working parties. Regt HQ in Rendre	
2nd	Regt were attacked for instruction	
3rd	Military of importance to report	
4th to 7th	Relieved the 1/7 W.Y.Rt in trenches	Quiet month. Very few casualties
	Cold frosty weather. Except that the enemy shelled the old Fort nothing of importance occurred	
7th	Relieved by 1/7 W.Y.Rt & moved into Brigade Reserve at HUMBERCAMP where the unit remained until the 11th The 1/7 London Regt were relieved by the 2/4 on the 9th. Training & working parties	
11th	Relieved the 1/8 W.Y.Rt and unit were being relieved at night & 1/8th was refused. 2/4 Smith & 1/8 admitted to wounded & gassed based on a ref covered by chicancy & 7am by turning B front lines shortly in gun and infantry at the front returned as though casualties	
12th to 14th	At quiet time in trenches Enemy artillery rather quiet our gas operation	2/Lieuts REDHOUSE & FIRTH joined
15th	Released by 1/7 & moved into Bde Reserve at BAILLEULMONT	2/Lt M rejoined
16th to 19th	Remained in Bde Reserve. Found 450 men working parties continued training. The 2/12 Rt & 1/8 Rt were in the 185	
20th	The unit moved by march route to billets at IVERGNY & remained	2/Lieut JESSOP joined
24th	Unit moved by march route to billets at BOURQUEMAISON	2/Lieut JESSOP left 6pm 62 M.E.
25th	do HERICOURT	2/Lieut GRIER left 6 Jan 12 WY
26th	do GAUCHY & LATOUR	
27th	do St FLORIS	
28th	do VIEILLE CHAPELLE	

Vol 19

19 C
10 sheets

SECRET.

WAR DIARY.

OF

1/8th Batt. West Yorks Regt

FOR

March 1917.

WAR DIARY
or
INTELLIGENCE SUMMARY.
(Erase heading not required.)

Army Form C. 2118.

Instructions regarding War Diaries and Intelligence Summaries are contained in F.S. Regs., Part II. and the Staff Manual respectively. Title pages will be prepared in manuscript.

Hour, Date, Place	Summary of Events and Information	Remarks and references to Appendices
1.3.17 VIELLE CHAPELLE and TRENCHES	The battalion moved from VIELLE CHAPELLE at 8am via CROIX BARBÉE, ROUGE CROIX, and RUE DU BACQUEROT to the trenches at N.24.d.57.17 to N.13.c.46 relieving the 1/5 LONDON REGT (LONDON RIFLE BRIGADE) Disposition of Battalion A Co on the right, B Co centre, D Co on the left, C Co in Support. Bn BEND POST. Total strength of Battalion 37 officers 932 O.R. Return strength 28 officers 905 " The trenches were found to be in very poor repair.	REFERENCE Trench Map AUBERS 36 S.W.1 Edition 8A 1/10,000
2.3.17 TRENCHES	In the trenches - Vergnies (?) Our patrols out all along Battalion front. A hostile patrol of 10-12 men were seen and on our patrol approaching retired to our lines. 2 Lt J. ILLINGWORTH left to be Bomb. Major of LAVENTIE. In the trenches. Normal patrols out at night but nothing to report.	
3.3.17 do		
4.3.17 do	Very quiet during the day. Small working parties detailed to keep trenches in repair. At night enemy parties out strengthening wire along Battalion front. Our patrol of 1 officer and 12 men encountered an enemy patrol of about 36. The latter were split up into three parties. One party on either flank and 5 men in the centre. Owing to the enemy patrol being able to take cover behind a dyke and the difficulty of getting to the enemy owing to mud, our patrol was able to drive back into their lines. 2nd Lt SMITH MC left for 146 Infantry Brigade.	

Army Form C. 2118.

WAR DIARY
or
INTELLIGENCE SUMMARY.
(Erase heading not required.)

Hour, Date, Place	Summary of Events and Information	Remarks and references to Appendices
5.3.17 TRENCHES	Lt Col. HUDSON D.S.O. returns from leave and took over command of the Battalion from Major LONGBOTTOM.	
6.3.17 do	In the trenches. Usual patrols out at night, but nothing to report. In the trenches. Usual patrols out, Minenwerfers out strengthening wire.	
7.3.17 do LAVENTIE	Battalion relieved in the trenches by 1/7 West Yorkshire Regt. and proceeded to billets in LAVENTIE. Relief completed without incident.	
8.3.17 do	The companies carried on with Inter-Company Economy and Battn. A party of 1 officer and 525 O.R. worked on Corps Winter Station. Capt W.H.BROOKE M.C. left to go to 146 Infantry Brigade.	
9.3.17 do	The Companies carried on with training on very limited training area. A Co. inspected by O.C. 4 sections of sappers sent to Brigade School for training in Lewis Guns. Also 5 sections of bombers sent to same place for training. Major S.S.SYKES rejoined the Battalion from sick leave and took over the duties of 2nd in Command. Working party of 1 officer and 20 O.R. at Corps Winter Stn.	

(73989). W4141—463. 400,000. 9/14. H.&J.Ltd. Forms/C. 2118/10.

WAR DIARY
or
INTELLIGENCE SUMMARY.
(Erase heading not required.)

Army Form C. 2118.

Hour, Date, Place	Summary of Events and Information	Remarks and references to Appendices
10.3.17 LAVENTIE	Usual training carried on by Companies. B Company inspected by O.C. Rifles by A.D. Corps inspects the Armourer Sergeant. Working party of 1 officer and 25 O.R. at Corps Wireless Pru. Simple tactical scheme carried out by officers under O.C. Concert given in the Recreation Room at 5.30 p.m.	
11.3.17 do	Capt T.E. APPLEYARD left for G.H.Q Senior Sims "A" Course. Church parade, att rpt 300 attended. After service Companies marched past General Commanding Division. (General PERCEVAL C.B. D.S.O) Companies inspected in billets by O.C.	
12.3.17 do	2nd Lt BELLHOUSE left for course of Divisional Lewis Company practiced new formation of attack. Moved running party to Pinches Post. Shr. Concert in the Recreation Room at 5.30 p.m.	
13.3.17 do and TRENCHES	The Battalion relieved the 1/7 Worcestershire Regt in the trenches FAUQUISSART SECTOR. Disposition of Battalion A Co on the right, B. Co Centre, D Co on the left and C Co in Support. 2nd Lt. H.R.P. WRIGHT rejoined the Battalion from sick leave. LIEUT W.H.C. JEFFCOCK joined the Battalion and took up his duties as Signalling Officer.	

WAR DIARY or INTELLIGENCE SUMMARY.

(Erase heading not required.)

Army Form C. 2118.

Hour, Date, Place	Summary of Events and Information	Remarks and references to Appendices
14.3.17 TRENCHES	Trench conditions normal. Usual patrols out along Battalion front. Enemy trenches (front line) as usual occupied.	
15.3.17 do	2nd Lt J.C. CHADWICK left for XI Corps Sniping Course. Usual MTRs and patrols carried out.	
16/17.3.17 do	do	
18.3.17 do	Capt J.E.A. APPEARED returned from Lewis Gun Course. 2nd Lt C.F.J. TAFT left from Divisional School Musketry Course. Patrol reached enemy lines M24d 96 and found French trenches and full of funerals. Very quiet during the day. 2nd Lt SMITH M.G. returned to Battalion from 148th Infantry Brigade.	
19.3.17 SUPPORT RED HOUSE and LAVENTIE	Battalion relieved in trenches by 1/7 West Yorkshire Regt. and moved into Support Battalion H.Q. RED HOUSE N6a 2.9. At B. Coy in billets LAVENTIE. C Co 3 Platoons DEAD END POST. 1 Platoon PIBANTIN POST. D.Co. 1 Platoon WANGERIE POST. 1 Platoon WASSELOT POST 1 Platoon HOUGOUMONT POST Ration carrying parties provided.	
20.3.17 do	Companies in LAVENTIE carried on with interior economy. Working and ration parties provided, requiring 260 men. 3rd Lt A.H. RAMSDEN relinquishes parties provided, requiring 200 men. 20 command a company acting rank of Captain on ceasing to command a company from 10.3.17 2nd Lt BELLHOUSE relinquish temporary rank of Lieut on ceasing B.E.F. 6.2.17	

Army Form C. 2118.

WAR DIARY
or
INTELLIGENCE SUMMARY.
(Erase heading not required.)

Instructions regarding War Diaries and Intelligence Summaries are contained in F. S. Regs., Part II. and the Staff Manual respectively. Title pages will be prepared in manuscript.

Hour, Date, Place	Summary of Events and Information	Remarks and references to Appendices
21.3.17 RED HOUSE and LAVENTIE	Companies in LAVENTIE bathed and medically inspected. Usual morning and ration parties = 295 men	
22.3.17 do	A & B Coys moves from billets in LAVENTIE and relieves C & D Coys in Support Posts. A Co taking over from C Co and B Co from D. Usual morning parties — 289 men	
23.3.17 do	C & D Coys moved into billets vacated by A & B Coys with interior economy, baths and medically inspected. Games in usual morning and ration parties/ movies = 293 men	
24.3.17 do	2ND LT H.R.D WRIGHT left to take up duties as Corps Trench Registration Officer. Companies in LAVENTIE carried on with training.	
25.3.17 do	At 3.20 am night of the 24/25 a heavy bombardment caused the Companies in the Support line (A & B Coys) to stand to. Their subsequent disposal to be a culmination by the Division on our left. The Companies stood to an 3.50 am	
25.3.17 do TRENCHES	The battalion relieves the 17 Warwickshire Regt in the trenches — The relief was held up for about an hour owing to heavy enemy howl. mortars in the front line and by ELGIN and ERITH C.T.S. Disposition of Battalion. A Co on the right. B Co Centre, D Co on the left and C Co in Support. Heavy shelling on ELGIN and parts of our outgoing the front during the day. 2ND LT J.C. CHADWICK rejoins battalion from XI Corps Infantry Course.	

WAR DIARY
or
INTELLIGENCE SUMMARY
(Erase heading not required.)

Army Form C. 2118.

Hour, Date, Place	Summary of Events and Information	Remarks and references to Appendices
25.3.17 TRENCHES	From 5 pm to 6.30 pm the enemy shelled the part of the line from (M24 b 7 8 to N 30 1 2) from 7 pm to 10.30 pm NORTH ELGIN ST gas shells gas. The hostile shelling ceased. At about 11.15 pm a party of about 40 of the enemy endeavoured to creep on our front trenches immediately north of BEDFORD R⁰ (M24 b 78). They threw many bombs but were driven back by our rifle fire. The enemy appears to have separated into small parties as one of them was attacked by our patrol, and a Lewis gun opened on them. Our casualties were 2 killed (including 2/Lt J.E.CHADWICK) and 7 wounded. Most of these casualties were caused by enemy machine gun fire from the German front line. The enemy left 3 dead, and three must have been wounded, wounded by our flanking fire and Lewis guns. We secured some important information from letters and note books found on the enemy dead and they left behind them a large number of bombs, two infernal machines, wire cutters, very pistols	

WAR DIARY
or
INTELLIGENCE SUMMARY.
(Erase heading not required.)

Army Form C. 2118.

Hour, Date, Place	Summary of Events and Information	Remarks and references to Appendices
25.3.17 TRENCHES	The night was very dark, rendering quick movement almost impracticable. In connection with the attempts of the enemy to enter our trenches, the following message was received from the 146 Infantry Brigade:- "The Divisional General congratulates the 1/5th Yorkshire Rgt on the following message: "The Divisional Commander wishes please at the man who mounted the German parapet last night was a man of information was and had been through the preliminary bombardment without delay, the plan he was upon it is an excellent sample of the best and boldest method of meeting an attack, and the execution shows coolness and determination on the part of all who were engaged."	

WAR DIARY
or
INTELLIGENCE SUMMARY.
(Erase heading not required.)

Army Form C. 2118.

Hour, Date, Place	Summary of Events and Information	Remarks and references to Appendices
26.3.17 TRENCHES	In the trenches. Very quiet throughout the day. Patrols out at night searching NO MAN'S LAND for any further casualties regarding the raid of the previous night. A number of letters and papers found on one of the enemy dead.	
27/28/9/3/17 do	In the trenches. Parties working on the trenches repairing same. Patrols out at night, but no signs of the enemy were found.	
30/3.17 do	2nd Lt BELLHOUSE returned from 49th Divisional School Course. In the trenches. Heavy rain at stand to. Quiet throughout the day. Two patrols out at night. No trace of the enemy could be found in their front line.	
31.3.17 LAVENTIE	The Battalion was relieved in the trenches by 1/7 West Yorkshire Regt and proceeded to billets in LAVENTIE. Every man in the Battalion was given clean clothing and Chaplin blankets. 2nd Lt RAMSDEN admitted to hospital. 2nd Lt DEDMAN proceeded to ABBEVILLE on a Transport Course. 2nd Lt TAFT returned from Musketry Instructors Course at Divisional School. Total strength at end of month. 35 Officers 905 O.R. Casualties for month. Killed in action 1 Offr. 15 O.R. wounded	Maj. I. Carleton A/Lt. Col. 1/8 W. Rid.

Vol 20

20 C
10 sheets

SECRET.

WAR DIARY.

OF

18th Batt West Yorks Reg^t

FOR

April 1917.

Army Form C. 2118.

WAR DIARY
INTELLIGENCE SUMMARY.
1/8 WEST YORKSHIRE REGT. APRIL 1917

(Erase heading not required.)

Hour, Date, Place	Summary of Events and Information	Remarks and references to Appendices
1.4.17 LAVENTIE	In Brigade Reserve and billets at LAVENTIE. All Companies carried on with Interior Economy. A party of 2 officers and 120 O.R. worked on the wire in the line from 7pm to 1am. 2.4.17. 2nd Lt C.F.J. TAFT wounded and admitted to hospital. Total strength of Battalion 34 Officers 905 O.R.	Ref: Map AUBERS 36 SW1 1/10,000
2.4.17 do	Training in LAVENTIE. Morning bathing parties provided 2 officers and 98 O.R.	
3.4.17 do	2nd Lt TURNER proceeded to 49th Divisional Musketry Instructors Course. Training. Morning bathing parties provided 2 officers 98 OR. 2nd Lt LENNOX handed over from D Co. to B Co.	
4.4.17 do	Training. Morning bathing parties provided 2 officers 98 O.R. Regimental Concert held in Recreation Room LAVENTIE at 5pm.	
5.4.17 do	Carried on with usual training. Morning bathing parties provided. 2 officers 108 O.R.	

WAR DIARY
INTELLIGENCE SUMMARY

(Erase heading not required.)

Army Form C. 2118.

Hour, Date, Place	Summary of Events and Information	Remarks and references to Appendices
5.4.17 LAVENTIE	The following message received from the Corps Commander (First Army) in connection with the successful raid on our trenches on the night of the 25/26th March:— "The Army Commander wishes that his appreciation should be conveyed to the O.C. and all ranks of the 1/8th West Yorkshire Regt. for the successful manner in which the recent raid was carried out & conducted."	
6.4.17 C/o A/S TRENCHES M.24.3. to N.13.2	The Battalion relieves the 1/7 WEST YORKSHIRE REGT in the trenches (FAUQUISSART SECTION) D Co on the right. C. Co Centre. B Co. left. A Co Support. The relief was completed without incident. Patrols out during night but no sign of the enemy was seen for hours.	
7.4.17 TRENCHES	The usual patrol out at night, but nothing to report. 2nd Lt WORSLEY proceeds to 49th Divisional School	
8.4.17	The enemy put over about a dozen trench mortar shells on our Centre Co (M.24.4.) The usual patrols out at night but nothing to report	

WAR DIARY
or
INTELLIGENCE SUMMARY.
(Erase heading not required.)

Army Form C. 2118.

Hour, Date, Place	Summary of Events and Information	Remarks and references to Appendices
8.4.17 TRENCHES M.24.3 to N.13.2	2ND LT SEYMOUR returned from 49th Divisional School	
9.4.17 do	Slight enemy trench mortar activity on our front about 8.30 a.m. At night a strong patrol made an extensive reconnaissance of the GERMAN line. They found the front line unoccupied, and in many places waterlogged. No sounds were heard. 2ND LT. J.W. RAISTRICK joined the Battalion and took up his duties as Signalling Officer.	
10.4.17 do	During a snowstorm in the afternoon 2/Lt APPLEYARD and Sgt COULSON of D Co. made their way across to the GERMAN line to investigate certain poles seen sticking up out of enemy trench about M.24.d.7.4 a patrol went out at night to complete the investigation, and from the information gained the conclusion was formed that the poles are used to mark the place from which Very lights were fired and also a direction mark for TMs. Our patrol took the pole on down	

WAR DIARY
INTELLIGENCE SUMMARY.
(Erase heading not required.)

Army Form C. 2118.

Instructions regarding War Diaries and Intelligence Summaries are contained in F.S. Regs., Part II. and the Staff Manual respectively. Title pages will be prepared in manuscript.

Hour, Date, Place	Summary of Events and Information	Remarks and references to Appendices
11.4.17 TRENCHES N24.3 to N13.2	Slight enemy trench mortaring on our front. Patrols went out at night but had nothing to report.	
12.4.17 In Support	The battalion was relieved by the 1/7 West Yorkshire Regt in the trenches, and went into Support with HQ at RED HOUSE (M6d.2.1) A and B Coys garrisoned the posts along the Rue Bacquerot and C and D Coys proceeded to billets in LAVENTIE.	
13/14.4.17 do	Morning parties provided at nights = 285 O.R. The battalion fully employed in supplying working parties. Total by day 169, by night 284.	
15.4.17 do	Inter Company relief. C and D Coys moved up from LAVENTIE and took over the posts in the RUE BACQUEROT from A and B Cos, the latter companies proceeding to billets in LAVENTIE	
16.4.17 do	2nd Lt TURNER returned from 49th Divl Musketry Course (14th) Morning parties provided Average wg 363 O.R. 2nd Lt CALLAGHAN proceeded to Third Army School	
16.4.17 do		
17.4.17 do	The usual morning parties provided avg 453 OR per day.	

WAR DIARY
INTELLIGENCE SUMMARY.
(Erase heading not required.)

Army Form C. 2118.

Hour, Date, Place	Summary of Events and Information	Remarks and references to Appendices
17.4.17 SUPPORT	The following awards have been made. Military Cross to 2ND LT W.F. WORSLEY D.Co. Military Medal " 1757 L/Cpl G.A. BLAYMIRE do " 2750 Rfn F WEBSTER do	
18.4.17 TRENCHES N24.3 to N13.2	For gallantry and devotion to duty in repelling an attack by the enemy on our trenches on the night of 25/26th March 1917. The battalion relieves the 1/7 West Yorkshire Regt in the trenches.	
18.4.17 do	In the trenches. Enemy very quiet. Listening patrols went out in front of our right and left Coys. but no sign of the enemy was seen or heard.	
19.4.17 do	From 4.30 p.m. to 6.30 p.m. about 30 heavy T.M.s fell on our lines. About 9.45 p.m. a salvo of light T.M.s caught our wiring party about N13.0 2.3, causing two slight casualties.	
20.4.17 do	2ND LT F.W. SMITH M.C. proceeds to XI Corps H.Q. to take up duties as Intelligence Officer for Corps Heavy Artillery. 2ND LT S.M. WEAVER rejoins from Brigade Comptche Co.	

Army Form C. 2118.

WAR DIARY
or
INTELLIGENCE SUMMARY.
(Erase heading not required.)

Instructions regarding War Diaries and Intelligence Summaries are contained in F. S. Regs., Part II. and the Staff Manual respectively. Title pages will be prepared in manuscript.

Hour, Date, Place	Summary of Events and Information	Remarks and references to Appendices
20.4.17 TRENCHES N24.3 to N13.2	Slight enemy trench mortar activity on our front line. Patrol went out at night and examined the enemy front line at N24 and 9.6. No movement was heard or seen.	
21.4.17 do	Enemy quiet during the day. Several patrols went out at night along our front, but there was nothing of importance to report. 2ND LT J.H. COLLINS joined the Battalion and posted to B.Co.	
22.4.17 do	A patrol went out at night and reconnoitred CLARA TRENCH in the vicinity of N.19 a 5 7. Tournes of enemy were heard, but the party could not the locate. Another patrol of 3 ny. on getting out of our line were seen from the direction of N24dR5, 2ND LT W.E. WORSLEY M.C. returns from 49th Divisional School.	
23.4.17	A patrol explored the GERMAN front line at M 3 and 6.3 which was found to be unoccupied but well protected. On this point the enemy put over about ten hungers gas shells onto our front line.	

(73989) W4141—463. 400,000. 9/14. H.&J.Ltd. Forms/C. 2118/10.

WAR DIARY
INTELLIGENCE SUMMARY.
(Erase heading not required.)

Army Form C. 2118.

Hour, Date, Place	Summary of Events and Information	Remarks and references to Appendices
24.4.17 TRENCHES N24.3 to N13.2 LAVENTIE	The Battalion was relieved in the trenches by 1/4 WEST YORKSHIRE REGT and proceeded to billets in LAVENTIE. During the afternoon all men commenced from trenches had a bath and clean change of underclothing.	
25.4.17 do	The day was devoted to interior economy and general cleaning up. In the afternoon a Platoon of A Co under 2nd LT TURNER carried out a demonstration of the "Platoon in attack" before the G.O.C. Brigade. 2nd LT DEDMAN returned from Transport Course at ABBEVILLE.	
26.4.17 do	Training of all available men in the Battalion carried out on various fields near LAVENTIE. Special attention given to the Coy and Platoon in the attack, and the training of the Rifle Grenade sections, and economy drill. 2nd LT S.N. HUGHES joined the Battalion and posted to C. Co.	
27.4.17 do	Training on as above.	
28.4.17 do	Church Parade at 2 pm. do.	
29.4.17 do	Lecture given by 2nd LT TEMPEST Brigade Intelligence Officer on recent Operations and more particularly the taking of VIMY RIDGE.	
30.4.17 TRENCHES	Battalion relieved the 1/4 WEST YORKSHIRE REGT in the trenches. The relief was carried out without any special	

WAR DIARY
INTELLIGENCE SUMMARY

Army Form C. 2118.

Hour, Date, Place	Summary of Events and Information	Remarks and references to Appendices
30.4.17 TRENCHES N24.3 to N13.2	incident except that one man was slightly wounded going in	
27.4.17 LAVENTIE	The following Officers N.C.Os and men of the Battalion proceeded to Merville, and were presented with the ribbons of the medals mentioned opposite their names by LT. GENERAL SIR R.C.B. HAKING, K.C.B. Commanding XI Army Corps. MAJOR S.S. SYKES, MILITARY CROSS. CAPT. H.R. LUPTON, do 2ND LT. F.W. SMITH, do 2ND LT. W.E. WORSLEY, do 3377 L.CPL. CUNLIFFE, MILITARY MEDAL 1757 " BLAYMIRE, do 2750 RFN WEBSTER, do. A detachment of 20 O.R. under Capt. E.F. WILKINSON, M.C. was furnished by C Co. and in this connection the following message was received from the H.Q. of the 49th Division:- "The G.O.C. [49th Division] has directed me to inform you that the Corps Commander has expressed his pleasure at the "appearance, soldierly bearing and smartness of the "detachment of the Division off on the Ceremonial Parade "at MERVILLE on the 27 inst."	
30.4.17 do	Total strength of Battalion 36 Officers, 906 O.R. Ration strength " " 29 " 747 " Casualties for the month = 1 Officer wounded (2ND LT TAFT) O.R.= 1 Killed, 7 wounded.	M.W. Argand Major 2/8 West Yorkshire 1/8 West Yorkshire

Army Form C. 2118.

Vol 21

WAR DIARY
INTELLIGENCE SUMMARY.
(Erase heading not required.)

1/8 West Yorkshire Regt — May 1917

21.C
25 sheets

Hour, Date, Place	Summary of Events and Information	Remarks and references to Appendices
1.5.17 TRENCHES M24 d 10.50 to N13 c 40.55	The battalion carries on the ordinary duties incidental to trench warfare. The enemy appear to be doing more wiring on their front line. Battalion strength Total 36 Officers 907 O.R. " Ration 29 " 750 " " Trench 24 " 640 "	Ref Map:— Aubers 36 SW1 Ed 8A 1/10000
2.5.17 06	A patrol of 1 Officer and 3 O.R. went out during the night of the 30/1st and found the enemy's front line about N19 a.5.8 occupied. At 3.20 am a heavy hostile barrage was put on neighbourhood of Elgin Post (M24 a.55) At 3.30 am a patrol of ours went from their position at N24 d 37 trying to reconnu and bombing going on on the left of the centre Co (M24 b.88) About this time 2 recon's barrage was put over on our front line and old support line in M24 b. and d, and at the same time a heavy protective M.G. barrage across No Man's Land on each flank of the raiders. No opens from n. well be here the enemy's front line. One of our Lewis gun teams saw a party of 5	

Army Form C. 2118.

WAR DIARY
INTELLIGENCE SUMMARY.
(Erase heading not required.)

1/8 WEST YORKSHIRE REGT

Hour, Date, Place	Summary of Events and Information	Remarks and references to Appendices
2.5.17 TRENCHES M24d 1050 to N13c 42.58	outside our wire but did not get far for fear of hitting our patrol which was returning by the same route. One of the party of 5 came up to our fence, and a Lewis Gunner, Rfn TALBOT shot one of them dead with his revolver. A hand to hand struggle then ensued and the German collapsed. A patrol was then sent out to reconnoitre on same and found one wounded German (N.C.O.) and one dead. Both were brought in and it was discovered that they belong to the 2nd Battalion, 6th BAVARIAN REGT, 6th Division. The identification being normal. The main party of the enemy had entered our trench a bit further up our trench and appear to have another 3 bombs and, bolted. About 30 bombs were picked up, and an unexploded Lewis mortar bomb among others was recovered. Our casualties - 6 wounded, none serious, 2 shell–pep. Two remained on duty.	

WAR DIARY

INTELLIGENCE SUMMARY.

Army Form C. 2118.

1/8 WEST YORKSHIRE REGT

Hour, Date, Place	Summary of Events and Information	Remarks and references to Appendices
2.5.17 TRENCHES M24d 10.50 to N13c 40.58	The wounded prisoner was taken to the 1/1 W.R. Field Ambulance and shortly afterwards was examined by the Intelligence Staff. He said he was 6. Bavarian N.C.O. (No.262) belonging to the 2nd Bttn 6th Bavarian Regt. He also stated that the 2nd Battalion of the 6th Bavarian Regt was in Reserve in AUBERS and the 1st Bttn in the trenches. Prisoners had heard that orders had been given to re-occupy the front line in this sector. He said it was not a "Sturm-truppe Raid" but a fighting patrol consisting of 8 men and 1 N.C.O. who came from reserve in AUBERS to obtain an identification. The prisoner was so badly wounded that it was impossible to extract further information from him and he died soon afterwards. Rfn TALBOT, above referred to, was awarded the Military Medal for gallantry and devotion to duty in the recess.	

Army Form C. 2118.

1/8 WEST YORKSHIRE REGT

WAR DIARY
INTELLIGENCE SUMMARY
(Erase heading not required.)

Hour, Date, Place	Summary of Events and Information	Remarks and references to Appendices

3.5.17 TRENCHES
N24 d 10.50 to
N 13 c 40.58
	The enemy put over about 100 4.2's during the afternoon in the neighbourhood of the O.Ps at N.18 a 2.1. The loopholes of one O.P. was damaged.
	
	During the morning the following detachment of the R.E.F. arrived for 48 hours instruction
	5 officers and 171 O.R. No 2 Coy 24th Regt
	1 " 47 " 23rd Regt
	24 O.R. and 26 horses were attached to the transport.
	The detachment was accompanied by Lieut LEAH Interpreter.
	The following changes in organization were completed to-day for a Special purpose. A composite company was formed comprising the following O.R. from A Co. 19
	    " " B " 34
	    " " C " 23
	    " " D " 26
	Capt E.F. WILKINSON M.C. in command, the other officers being 2nd Lt KEMP, 2nd Lt MORTIMER & 2nd Lt FIRTH	

Army Form C. 2118.

WAR DIARY
INTELLIGENCE SUMMARY.

(Erase heading not required.)

1/8 WEST YORKSHIRE REGT

Hour, Date, Place	Summary of Events and Information	Remarks and references to Appendices
4.5.17 TRENCHES M24d 10.50 to N13C 42 55	Nothing of importance to relate. Patrols went out at night for listening purposes only.	
5.5.17 do	The detachment of Rangers, attached to the Battalion for instruction since the 3.5.17 left for billets in LAVENTIE. During their attachment the men showed themselves to be quite keen to learn. Listening patrols went out at night.	
6.5.17 do	The Battalion was relieved in the trenches by the 1/7 WEST YORKSHIRE REGT, and proceeded to the Posts on the RUE DU BACQUEROT as Support. H.Q. RED HOUSE. 8A and B Companies proceeded to billets in LAVENTIE. Composite Co. at PICANTIN and DEAD END POST. B. Co. at MASSELOT, HOUGOUMONT, WANGERIE, and LONEWY POSTS. At night the Battalion furnished working parties of 2 Officers 211 O.R.	

Army Form C. 2118.

WAR DIARY
INTELLIGENCE SUMMARY.
(Erase heading not required.)

1/8 WEST YORKSHIRE REGT.

Hour, Date, Place	Summary of Events and Information	Remarks and references to Appendices
7.5.17 SUPPORT HQ. at W6d 2.1	The men of A and D Coys held fetes in LAVENTIE were in the billets during the morning. Morning barrier were hit by shells of 5 Officers and DR. 2nd Lt A.N. RAMSDEN left for Divisional gun "A" Centre at LETOUQUET. A raid was carried out on the enemy's trenches at 9.40 pm on the night of the 7.5.17 under command of Capt E.F.WILKINSON, M.C. and 2nd Lt W.G. KEMP second in command. 2nd Lt ENFIRTH and 2nd Lt A.L. MORTIMER were in command of flank parties. The total strength of the raiding party was 4 Officers and 104 OR including 1 Corporal and 1 man of the R.E. 146 Infantry Brigade Operations Orders No 48 attached 1/8 West Yorkshire Regt. " No 20 " 148 Infantry Brigade (on the right) also arranged a demonstration. Parties of our scouts as —— The O.C. Raid, Capt E.F.WILKINSON, M.C. reported as follows on the operation:— "We were ready in our front line by 9.20 pm when we moved out into the assembly position which was reached by 9.37½ pm (Zero – 2½ minutes). The bridges were put into position by Zero – 10 minutes.	Appendix A " B " C

Army Form C. 2118.

WAR DIARY
or
INTELLIGENCE SUMMARY.
(Erase heading not required.)

1/8 WEST YORKSHIRE REGT

Hour, Date, Place	Summary of Events and Information	Remarks and references to Appendices
7.5.17 SUPPORT (HQ AT M6 A 2.1)	"At Zero the mopping party crossed the bridge and formed up on the far side of the dyke. Meanwhile other parties crept in parties to within 25 yards of the barrage which was very accurate – all on our front. At Zero plus 3 minutes our guns lifted to the German front line, moving something in getting through the wire. Meanwhile the two flank parties reached their positions exactly as arranged. No. 1 party found no machine gun. Forward parties reached the front line at the top of DORA TRENCH. A Boche post was found taking refuge in a dugout. One prisoner was taken. I gave orders for the front line to be systematically searched before going forward, and it was found to be an empty, battered version of trenches including our torpedo party, we went forward to reconnoitre the mopping up/support/reserve lines. The Boches then opened the German barrage and mortars etc. etc. coming with 3 light trench mortars etc."	

WAR DIARY
INTELLIGENCE SUMMARY

1/8 WEST YORKSHIRE REGT

Army Form C. 2118.

Hour, Date, Place	Summary of Events and Information	Remarks and references to Appendices
7.4.17 SUPPORT (HQ M6d 2.1)	what appeared to be Very lights & canisters. It extremely doubtful that they were any enemy Vereans. I gave orders to the reaching of the German front line to be completed, and several runners to hqrs. shelter were found, Sans bombs, Being satisfied that no more Germans were in front line, and the new objective having been certained. I gave orders to withdraw at 16.5 pm. This was accomplished — all casualties removed except Lyng 2nd Lt Kemp to stop the barrage as I thought the wounded at the North side then lying in No Mans Land. This was justified as the Germans promptly lengthened range onto our CTs making it to bring in our casualties. Parties all returned to front line & reported to Capt A R Lupton MC at Report Centre, and then handed in "g" line. Casualties 1 OR killed 4 OR wounded all brought in. Arrived at 10.25 pm. Covering parties in were in at 10.35 pm.	

Army Form C. 2118.

WAR DIARY
of
INTELLIGENCE SUMMARY.
(Erase heading not required.)

1/8 WEST YORKSHIRE REGT

Instructions regarding War Diaries and Intelligence Summaries are contained in F. S. Regs., Part II. and the Staff Manual respectively. Title pages will be prepared in manuscript.

Hour, Date, Place	Summary of Events and Information	Remarks and references to Appendices
7.5.17 "SUPPORT" (HQ M6d 2.1)	"Communication through out was excellent and 1/7 Bn WEST YORKSHIRE REGT rendered the line men ranks very prompt & valuable assistance." "The Machine Gun barrage was very accurate and intense." "The behaviour of all ranks was excellent." Enemy Machine Gun fire began 8 minutes after 300 from Gun about N26a 9.7 and was continuous for about 6 minutes. Machine Gun fire began again at 9.55 pm, two guns firing from about same direction in bursts on & two minutes. Enemy artillery began at 9.40 pm 12 minutes — whizz bangs on strong line near ERITH STREET and heavier stuff on BATTLELOY ROAD from ELGIN ST to FAUQUISSART ROAD. Enemy artillery ceased at 10.2 pm. Enemy all afraid to fire from FME SALOME direction. Flares occasionally seen. 1st Red Very Lights were sent up from Bn front line near BERTHA TRENCH at 9.45 pm. 1st Red Very Lights seen up from 9.45 pm to 9.57 pm when 3 Green Lights, 1 Red 3 Green, 3 Green, were sent up in quick succession from bearing 97° (true) from CONNENT O.P. probably from HQ at N20 b.3.5. The German artillery has been on for 5 minutes before the Verey lights went up.	

Army Form C. 2118.

WAR DIARY
or
INTELLIGENCE SUMMARY.
(Erase heading not required.)

1/8 WEST YORKSHIRE REGT

Hour, Date, Place	Summary of Events and Information	Remarks and references to Appendices
7.5.17 SUPPORT (HBakM6a2.1)	The result of the raid was that one prisoner was captured (slightly wounded) and altogether two killed. The post captured appears to have been an isolated one. Particulars of the examination of Prisoner captured of the 262 R.I.R. 79th Res Division is attached as —	Appendix D " E
	In connection with the raid the following wires were received from G.O.C. 49th Division:- "G.O.C. congratulates you on recent of your raid. The Corps Commander also is very pleased to hear of your success and the identification obtained of 79th Div is a fine one." "G.O.C. Division congratulates Major Sykes and Capt Wilkinson."	
8.5.17 do	My half Battn nr LAVENTIE A and D Coy moved up to the Rue du Bacquerot, and the Batty dispositions were as follows A Co. HOBCOUMONT, MASSELOT and APPLE HOUSE. B " WANGERIE and LONELY C " ROAD BEND POST D " PICANTIN and DEAD END POST.	

Army Form C. 2118.

WAR DIARY
INTELLIGENCE SUMMARY.
(Erase heading not required.)

1/8 WEST YORKSHIRE REGT

Hour, Date, Place	Summary of Events and Information	Remarks and references to Appendices
8.5.17 SUPPORT (H.Q. M6c1 2.1)	Working parties furnished — 5 Officers 350 O.R. 2nd Lt. Jeffery and 21 O.R. left for First Army Rest Camp	
9.5.17 do	Usual working parties provided — 5 Officers 350 O.R. Lt Col R.A. Hudson D.S.O. returned from 146 Inf/Bde as took war command	
10.5.17 do	Usual working parties provided — 5 Officers 400 O.R. The 4 Officers and 102 new army Officers attached to 4 companies for a week returned to their Companies	
11.5.17 do	An unusual amount of shelling took place between 2 p.m and 4.30 p.m. One of the shells fell in the vicinity of DEAD END POST, killing one Corporal and wounding 6 O.R.	
12.5.17 TRENCHES N13c42.58 — N 30 05.85	Working parties provided — 5 Officers 400 O.R. The Battalion relieved the 1/5 West Yorkshire Regt in the trenches in the left Sub-Sector (FAUQUISSART II) C Co. on the Right A Co. Centre B Co Left. D Co. Support. The relief was completed without incident.	
13.5.17 do	Very quiet. Listening patrols sent out at night but had nothing to report. 2nd Lt. J.C.H. Collins left for XI Corps Infantry School Major d'Infanterie Horacio S. de Moraes Ferreira Off REF. left.	

Army Form C. 2118.

WAR DIARY
INTELLIGENCE SUMMARY.
(Erase heading not required.)

18 WEST YORKSHIRE REGT

Instructions regarding War Diaries and Intelligence Summaries are contained in F.S. Regs., Part II. and the Staff Manual respectively. Title pages will be prepared in manuscript.

Hour, Date, Place	Summary of Events and Information	Remarks and references to Appendices
14.5.17. TRENCHES N13c 49.58 to N8d 05.85	Nothing of importance to record. Enemy very quiet. Listening patrols out, but nothing to report. A patrol from C. Coy. entered the German lines about N13d 70.60. The trenches were found to be badly knocked about and flooded.	
15.5.17 do	2ND LT A.M. RAMSDEN returned from leave. Enemy "A" Coy. Whilst our patrol was out a hostile M.G. fired from Enemy front line near N14a 9.6. Lt Col R/A HUDSON DSO took over command of 146 Infantry Brigade vice Major R.S.SUGDEN MC who rejoined from attached to record. Very quiet day, and nothing of importance to record.	
16.5.17 do	A patrol of 2 officers and 7 O.R. reconnoitred the enemy front line about N8d 4.3. The ground was found to be much cut up by shell holes and waterlogged. No signs of work on the German line at this point. Another patrol encountered a hostile covering party about N13d 8.7 but owing to the difficulty of crossing the dykes could not outflank them. During the night several routes across NoMANS LAND for our reconnaissance reconnoitred	
17.5.17 do	Nothing of importance to record	

Army Form C. 2118.

WAR DIARY
INTELLIGENCE SUMMARY.
(Erase heading not required.)

1/8 WEST YORKSHIRE REGT

Hour, Date, Place	Summary of Events and Information	Remarks and references to Appendices
18.5.17 TRENCHES N13 d 42.58 to N8 d 05 85 LAVENTIE	The battalion was relieved in the trenches by the 1/5 West Yorkshire Regt and proceeded to billets in LAVENTIE. In the afternoon A & B Coys were bathed, and men of B Co inoculated.	
19.5.17 do	All boys carried on with Interior Economy and men of A Co were inoculated. About 3pm the enemy started shelling LAVENTIE. Very high velocity which caused one ————— feet up. The Battalion H.Q. Mud 73.10 kysing 2 nd Lt J W RAISTRICK. The Battalion then evacuated the town until about 4.30 p.m. No Cas and no other casualties. 2 nd Lt J H COLLINS awarded ~ ^ Courage at the X1 Corps Infantry School was admitted to Hosp. sick & wounded at 6320 of 17.	
20.5.17 do	At 3.30 am the battalion moved outside the Cd between M5c and N11d in view of an Artillery retaliation on AUBERS at 4.30 am. Battalion H.Q. now was a little S of LAVENTIE E. POST M5c 7090. Morning was spent in view of the field until 1.30 pm. When the battalion returned to LAVENTIE. In view of a possible shelling of LAVENTIE by the enemy the Battalion H.Q. Co A Co (inoculated) moved out of the town to the field as above. H.Q. being	

Army Form C. 2118.

WAR DIARY
INTELLIGENCE SUMMARY.
(Erase heading not required.)

1/8 WEST YORKSHIRE REGT.

Hour, Date, Place	Summary of Events and Information	Remarks and references to Appendices
20.5.17 LAVENTIE	established at LAVENTIE E. Post. Nothing of importance occurred during the night	
21.5.17 do	2nd Lt L.W. Callaghan returned from First Army School. Capt H.R. Lupton MC, 2nd Lt A.M. Ramsden and 60 O.R. left for England on leave. The battalion carried on with training between 6.30am and 1.30pm. Special attention being given to musketry, the attack, practice and bayonet fighting	
22.5.17 do	do	
23.5.17 do	2nd Lt D.I. Currie left for course at 1yp? Army School. Camp D Coy ins on Lake during the afternoon. The battalion carried on with training as below.	
24.5.17 do	The battalion relieved the 1/7 West Yorkshire Regt in the front on the Rue Bacquerot line. At night the battalion furnished working parties of 2 Officers and 161 O.R.	
25.5.17 SUPPORT RED HOUSE	do	
26.5.17 do	do	
27.5.17 do	Working parties of 3 officers and 206 O.R.	

Army Form C. 2118.

WAR DIARY
INTELLIGENCE SUMMARY.
(Erase heading not required.)

1/8 WEST YORKSHIRE REGT

Hour, Date, Place	Summary of Events and Information	Remarks and references to Appendices
28/29.5.17 SUPPORT RED HOUSE	Nothing of importance to record. The usual working parties of 6 Officers and 350 O.R. supplied.	
30.5.17 do LAVENTIE	Between 7.30am & 8.30am there was heavy shelling of the Battery at M6C & 5 some of the shells (4.2 and 5.9) falling near Battalion HQ (Red House.) The Battalion was relieved in the posts on the Rue Bacquerot line by the 1/5 West Yorkshire Regt. the relief being completed at 1 pm. the Battalion on relief proceeded to billets in LAVENTIE. The Battalion carried on with ordinary Coy work. Ration strength 34 Officers 899 O.R. do 23 " 720 " Trench do 19 " 611 "	
31.5.17 do	Casualties for May 1917 Killed in Action 1 officer 2 O.R Wounded- remained at duty 16 " Wounded- 5- remained at duty 5 " Wounded- Accidental 1 officer 3 "	

M Rogan Lieut Adjt
1/8 West Yorkshire
p/ M Carforasack?

APPENDIX. A. to 146 Inf Bde. O.O. No 48

LEFT GROUP. R. F. A. ORDERS.

1. A/245. B/245, and C/245 Batteries will each have one Section of the 24th Battery attached.
   These Sections will report on the night May 3rd.1917.

2. Artillery programme will be as follows:-

A/245 Battery.

From ZERO to ZERO Plus 5.	3 Sections on front line between M.24.d.75.40. and N.19.c.15.75. Note. A Machine Gun is reported about M.24.d.80.45. This will be further reported on by Infantry.
From ZERO to ZERO Plus 7.	1 Section Enfilade Trenches from N.19.c.1.5. to N.19.c.5.2.
At ZERO plus 5 to ZERO plus 7.	The 3 Sections on front line will lift to Support Line.
At ZERO plus 7 to "CEASE FIRE"	All guns will lift on to BOX BARRAGE 3 Sections on Trench from N.19.c.35. 3.75. to N.19.c.25.10. 1 Section Enfilade Trench about N.19.c.4.1.

B/245 Battery.

ZERO to 'CEASE FIRE".	1 Section Enfilade Trenches from N.19.c.20.85. to N.19.c.5.7.
ZERO to plus 7.	3 Sections on Support Line from N.19.c.25.70 to N.19.c.1.5.
ZERO plus 7 to 'CEASE FIRE'.	Lift on to BOX BARRAGE on Trenches from N.19.c.25.70. to N.19.c.35.40.

C/245 Battery.

ZERO to 'CEASE FIRE'	1 Section Enfilade Trenches from M.24.d.7.4. to M.24.d.85.25.
ZERO to ZERO plus 7.	3 Sections on Support Line from N.19.c.1.5. to M.24.d.85.30.
ZERO plus 7 to 'CEASE FIRE'.	Lift on to BOX BARRAGE (MOTTES WAY) from M.24.d.85.30. to N.19.c.25.10.

B/245. Battery.

ZERO to 'CEASE FIRE'.	1 Section on TRIVELET. 1 Section. Trench Junctions. about N.19.c.35.10. (Ballistite) 1 Section about M.24.d.50.10. 1 Section Min.du PIETRE.

-2-

RATES OF FIRE.

18-pounders.

ZERO to ZERO plus 3. 4 rounds per gun per minute.
ZERO plus 3 to ZERO plus 7. 3 rounds per gun per minute.
ZERO plus 7 to ZERO plus 10. 2 rounds per gun per minute.
ZERO plus 10 to 'CEASE FIRE'. 1 round per gun per minute.

4.5" Howitzers.

Will fire at half the above rates.

....

Sections in enfilade will fire.   T.S.

On front line and support line.   P.S.

BOX BARRAGE.   H.E.

....

3. ZERO hour will be notified later.

4. Bursts of fire will take place an hour and half after the
raid, and at dawn.
    Batteries will fire 3 rounds Gun fire.

....

S E C R E T.   APPENDIX A   Copy No. 4

146th INFANTRY BRIGADE - OPERATION ORDER No.45.

Map Ref:- AUBERS. 36. S.W. 1.   6th May 1917.

1. The 1/8th Bn. W.York.R. will carry out a raid against the enemy trenches on the night 7/8th inst.

Point of Entry. 2. M.24.d.90.56. and M.24.d.80.50.

Object. 3. To capture prisoners and cause enemy casualties.

Strength of Party. 4. About 110.

Duration of Raid. 5. 20/30 Minutes stay in enemy's lines.

Time. 6. Zero hour 9-40.p.m.

Artillery Support. 7. Artillery programme. Appendix A attached.
In addition to this, Heavy Artillery will engage in counter battery work.

Machine Guns. 8. At zero, 146th Machine Gun Company will open a barrage as follows:-

6 guns - searching - M.24.d.70.20 to M.19.c.40.05.
6 guns -   do.   - N.19.c.40.60 to N.19.c.50.14.
2 guns -   do.   - N.19.a.52.15 to N.19.c.40.80.

2" Trench Mortars. 9. At zero 2" Trench Mortars will open fire as follows:-

6 guns covering DEVILS JUMP. N.19.a.5.5. to N.19.a.60.99
2 guns on BERTHA POST N.14.c.1.7.
Rate of fire - rapid from zero to zero plus 7 minutes
At zero plus 7, slow rate.

Light Trench Mortar Battery. 10. 146th Trench Mortar Battery will open fire at zero hour as follows:-
2 guns barrage from M.30.b.49 - M.30.b.25.60.
1 gun on N.13.d.central.
1 gun on N.14.c.90.97.
1 gun on N.19.a.2.4.
Rate of fire - rapid from zero to zero plus 7 minutes,
At zero plus 7, slow rate.

Flank Brigades. 11. (a) At zero hour 146th Brigade on right will co-operate with a Trench Mortar demonstration on dangerous points on enemy's line in M.30.a.
(b) At zero hour, 147th Brigade on left will co-operate with a Trench Mortar demonstration on enemy's line in N.8.d. and N.9.c.

12. 1/8th Bn. W.York.R. in left sub-sector will have a fighting patrol ready to seize any opportunity of creating a diversion or doing damage.

R.E. 13. 455th Field Coy. R.E. will arrange for two R.E. to accompany raiding party with Bangalore Torpedo, to blow gap in wire at N.19.c.60.50.

SYNCHRONIZATION. 14. Official time will be issued by the Brigade and a watch sent round to Left Group R.F.A. 148th. and 170th Brigades and to units, during the afternoon.

15. When all parties are in, O.C.Raid will telephone 'All Clear' to the R.F.A. who will then cease fire.

16. ACKNOWLEDGE.

         (Sgd) J.W.FISHER
              Captain.
       Brigade Major, 148th Infantry Brigade.

Issued at 3-30.p.m.

Copy No.1. 1/5th. Bn. W.York.R.
   2. 1/6th. -do-
   3. 1/7th. -do-
   4. 1/6th. -do-
   5. 1/8th. -do-
   6. 148th Machine Gun Coy.
   7. 148th Trench Mortar Battery.
   8. Staff Capt. 148th Brigade.
   9. O.C. No.2.Signal Section.
  10. 146th. Inf.Brigade.
  11. 170th. Inf.Brigade.
  12. D.T.M.O.
  13. 49th Division "G".
  14. 458th.Field Coy.R.E.
  15. Left Group R.F.A.
  16. War Diary.
  17. Retained.
  18. "
  19. "

APPENDIX B

OPERATION ORDERS NO. 20.   Copy No. 6

By MAJOR.S.S.SYKES, M.C. Commanding. 1/8th.West Yorkshire Regiment.

Reference AUBERS. 36.S.W. 1. Ed. 8a. 1/10,000.

1. The Battalion will carry out a Raid on the enemy's trenches on the night of 7/8th inst

2. Personnel. 4 Officers and 104 O.R.
Captain E.F.WILKINSON, M.C. in Command.

3. Object. To capture prisoners and cause enemy casualties.

4. Time. Zero hour ~~will be notified later.~~ 9.40 p.m.

5. Points of entry. M.24.d.9.6. and M.24.d.80.50.

6. Distribution of parties.

No.1.	1 N.C.O. & 8 men	Right flank party to deal with hostile M.G. at M.24.d.80.50.
No.2.	O.C.Party & 12 O.R.	Support Party.
No.3.	1 N.C.O. and 4 O.R.	Left flank post front line.
No.4.	1 N.C.O. and 8 O.R.	Right flank post 2nd.line.
No.5.	1 N.C.O. and 8 O.R.	Left flank post " "
No.6.	1 N.C.O. and 8 O.R.	Forward post " "
No.7.	1 N.C.O. and 4 O.R.) 2 R.E.)	Bangalore torpedo party.
No.8.	2/Lieut.KEMP, 2 N.C.Os. & 16 O.R.)	Attacking party.
No.9.	2/Lieut.MORTIMER, 1 N.C.O. & 12 men including L.G.)	Left covering party.
No.10.	2/Lieut.FIRTH, 1 N.C.O. & 12 men including L.G.)	Right covering party.

4 Officers. 10 N.C.Os. 94 men.

7. Scheme. The party assembles at DEAD END POST, after inspection, at zero minus 90 minutes.
They will move in separate parties up ELGIN C.T. at intervals of 100 yards, rendezvousing in our front line South of ELGIN STREET.
Parties Nos. 2, 7, 6, 5, 3, 8 in the order named will leave our lines at zero minus 20 minutes from point M.24.d.40.96.
Parties Nos. 4, 1, 8, in the order named will leave our lines at zero minus 20 minutes from point M.24.d.40.92.
These parties will take up positions in NO MAN'S LAND at :-
1. The first party comprising 1 and 4 assembling in old trench at M.24.d.6.8. - M.24.d.4.6.
2. Parties 2, 3, 5, 6, 7, 8, along dyke side running from North ELGIN STREET to M.24.d.75.82.
3. Parties Nos. 9 and 10 will leave our line at zero and take up positions at dyke side M.24.b.70.05. - M.24.b.48.20. and at dyke side M.24.d.50.48. - M.24.d.15.62. respectively.

O.C. "A" Company is responsible that the wire is cut at points of exit.

At zero, Artillery barrage opens on enemy front line and on 2nd line, and the party moves forward as near as possible to the point of entry M.24.d.9.6. except Nos. 1 and 4 parties, which move down the dyke side entering German front line at M.24.d.8.5.

- 2 -

At zero plus 5 minutes, barrage lifts from front line, the party enters front line trench, No.1 party entering at M.24.d.8.5. to deal with suspected M.Gun, and form a flank post. No.2 party remains at point of entry M.24.d.9.6. and No.3 party works north to N.19.c.0Y.72. where it forms a flank post.
05.

At zero plus 7 minutes, barrage lifts from 2nd line and completes box barrage round the DELTA. No. 7 party moves forward and blows gap in wire about N.19.c.00.50. and then returns and reports to No.2 party.

Immediately after the explosion parties Nos. 4, 5, 6, move forward, No.4 to form right flank post in 2nd line about M.24.d.98.40. No.5 left flank post at about N.19.c.13.55. No.6 forward post at N.19.c.10.45. Meanwhile party No.8 attacks the 2nd line between M.24.d.98.40. and N.19.c.13.55.

Party No.2 will be given 4 Bridges when in our front line and will be responsible for bridging the dyke at point about M.24.d.80.85.

8. Prisoners. Prisoners will be immediately sent back to No.2 party who will provide escort back to our front line and will be immediately sent down to Battalion H.Q. at RED HOUSE, an escort being found by the Company of the 7th.West Yorkshire Regiment in the line.

9. Signal. The signal to return will be sent round by Commander of No.8 party by RUNNERS, one to party No.6, one each along 2nd line to parties Nos.4 and 5, warning everybody on their way. Code word for return - WILTSHIRES - . All forward parties will immediately return under their party commanders, warning parties in German front line on their way and passing through them. The words RETIRE or WITHDRAW will NOT be used. Officers and N.C.Os. in charge of parties will see that their party is complete before leaving the German line.

All parties on re-entering our front line will report to the nearest garrison of front line who will at once inform O.C.Report Centre at M.24.b.4.1.

When all parties have reported in O.C.Raid will telephone through ALL CLEAR to Artillery, who will then cease fire.

10. Re-assembly. All parties will make their way at once to "B" Line between ELGIN and ERITH STREETS where they will re-assemble under O.C.Raid. Police of 7th.West Yorkshire Regiment on ERITH STREET and ELGIN STREET will turn all raiding party into "B" Line between ERITH and ELGIN STREETS.

11. Dress. Clean fatigue, hands and faces blackened, steel helmets, chin straps tight, square white patch on back below collar - Officers will wear double patch - streamer round helmet falling down the back.
Box Respirators in alert position, Field Dressing will be carried.
All papers, photos, identity discs, shoulder titles, and badges will be left behind.
Party No.2 and 50% of parties Nos.1, 3, 4, 5, 6, 7, 9, and 10 will carry Waterproof Sheets rolled up.

- 3 -

12.	Equipment.	Every man will take Rifle with Bayonet fixed and blackened, 10 rounds in magazine, 5 clips in pocket. Parties Nos. 1, 3, 4, 5, and 6, will carry 6 Mills Bombs per man in haversacks.
<u>Wire cutters</u>, will be carried by 25% of total party in left breast pocket, slung round the left shoulder.
<u>A Razor</u>, will be carried in the right breast pocket.

All Officers and N.C.Os. and No.6 party will wear light Body Shields.

4 men of No.5 party will carry one P.Bomb each for destroying the suspected dug-out at N.19.c.00.42.
Parties Nos. 1, 3, 4, and 5, will have luminous Sights on their Rifles. |
| 13. | Report Centre. | Report Centre under Captain H.R.LUPTON, M.C. will be formed in concrete dug-out at M.24.b.4.1. in our front line where telephone will be installed connected up with Centre Company H.Q. to Artillery. |
| 14. | Medical. | Dressing Stations at WINCHESTER POST, M.23.a.45.05. and WHITE HOUSE, M.12.c.25.35.

6 Stretcher Bearers about M.24.d.1.5. |
| 15. | Synchronization. | A Watch which has been set to correct time by O.C. LEFT GROUP R.F.A. will be sent to O.C.Raid, Trench Mortar Battery, Machine Gun Company, and Battalion H.Q. during the afternoon. |
| 16. | | ACKNOWLEDGE. |

Issued: 4 pm 7.5.17

Copy No. 1. 146 Infantry Brigade.
" 2. Captain E.F.WILKINSON.M.C.
" 3. 2/Lieut.KEMP.
" 4. 2/Lieut.MORTIMER & 2/Lt.FIRTH.
" 5. 1/7th.West Yorkshire Regt.
" 6. O.C. 458th.Field Coy.R.E.
" 7. War Diary.
" 8. Retained.

S E C R E T.   1/580.B.

1/5th Bn. W.York.R.
1/6th   -do-
1/7th   -do-   **APPENDIX C**
1/8th   -do-
146th Machine Gun Coy.
146th Trench Mortar Battery.
Left Group.R.F.A.
D.T.M.O.
....

        Reference Operation Order No.40. Para.11.a.

        148th Infantry Brigade have arranged as follows:-

        A party will go out to the CRATERS about M.30.a.6.7.and the enemy front line at M.30.a.7.4. with Stokes mortars and Mills Grenades with which they will supplement, in enfilade, our Stokes Mortar Barrage on the enemy front line M.30.b.2.5. to M.24.c.40.00.
        The party will also include a patrol who will be on the lookout for any of the enemy driven South by our barrage.

        The 146th. Stokes mortars will take on hostile Machine Gun which fires N.N.E. from M.30.a.40.14.

1/5/17.   (Sgd).   J.W.FISHER,
                                                            Captain.
                                        Brigade Major, 146th Infantry Brigade.

APPENDIX D

EXAMINATION of PRISONER of 262 R.R., 79th.
Res. Div. captured in FAUQUISSART
Sector. 7/5/17.

HISTORY - Prisoner is a German Pole and belongs to 2nd Bn. 262 R.R. He was called up on 24th November 1914, and spent two months in training at DOBARITZ and then joined the Regiment in RUSSIA and came to Western front with the Division in December.

METHOD OF HOLDING LINE - 2nd. Battalion in the trenches in the front of AUBERS, one company being in DELEVAL line. There are posts at intervals in the front line system; one at head of DORA trench which consists of four men by day and eight men by night; one sentry is on duty by day and two by night. As far as prisoner knows Very Lights are only sent up from these posts. There is another post about 250 yds to the South. He does not know position of post to the North. It is in another company's sector.

RELIEFS. - 262nd Reserve Regt. relieved 6th Bav.Regt. on night of 4/5th. Relief started from SANTES at 9 p.m. and was complete shortly after 12 midnight. Small advanced parties were sent forward a day or two before to act as guides.

H.Q. - Company H.Q. in DELEVAL line is a strong concrete dug-out. at N.25.a.65.65.

WIRE. - Wiring parties have been working in front of the new DELEVAL line. These parties work in two hour shifts generally 10 p.m. to 12 midnight, and 12 midnight to 2 a.m.

MACHINE GUNS. - New automatic rifle not yet received.

TRENCH MORTARS. - Prisoner thinks for the moment that there is a shortage of trained men for firing T.Ms. Trench Mortar School has been started at SANTES.

RATIONS, - Field Kitchens are in AUBERS. Carrying parties bring food into the trenches between 9 and 10 in the evening, and 3 and 4 in the morning. Prisoner does not know what time rations arrive at AUBERS.

GENERAL. - 79th. Res.Div. left VIMY area on 12th April 1917. 262nd R.R. was relieved in this area by 104th Regt. Division went into rest near COURTRAI, 262nd R.R. at SWEVEGHEM and spent fourteen days here. It then moved forward and detrained at WAVRIN and marched to SANTES.

....

Copy. **APPENDIX E**

Report on the examination of a wounded prisoner of
the II Battn., 262nd Res. Inf. Regt., 79th Res.Div.,
captured on the night of 7/8th May during a raid on
the enemy's trenches in M.24.a. (Sheet 36).

History.   Prisoner belongs to the 1914 class and was called up in
           Autumn 1914. He has served with the 262nd Res. Inf.Regt.
ever since.

Movements of 79th Res.Div.   The 79th Res.Division was relieved in
                             the VIMY area on 12/4/17 by the 111th
Division, the 262nd Res. Inf. Regt. being relieved by the 164th Inf.
Regt.

    The 262nd Res. Inf. Regt. entrained at 5 a.m. on 13/4/17, he is
not sure of the station, but believes it was BREBIERES. Travelling
via LILLE they detrained at SWEVEGHEM (5 miles S.E. of COURTRAI) at
about 2 p.m. on the same day. They rested at SWEVEGHEM for 14 days
and then moved by train to HAVRIN; from the latter place they marched
to rest billets at SANTES. On the night of the 4/5th May the 262nd
Res. Inf. Regt. relieved the 6th. Bav. Inf.Regt., 6th Bav. Division.

Order of Battle.   Prisoner has no definite information. He states
                   that Bavarians were still on his right and left on
7/5/17, but believes that by now the relief of the 6th Bav. Divn. by
the 79th Res.Divn. will have been completed. He had been told that
the 6th Bav. Divn. is going to be transferred to the ARRAS Sector. Men
of the 6th and 10th Bav. Inf. Regts. of the 6th Bav. Divn. were still
in SANTES on 8/5/17.

Company Strength.   The prisoner's company (7th) has a trench strength
                    of about 120 men with a full strength of about
150 men. There are two officers in the company. Since they left the
VIMY area the 79th. Res Divn. has received drafts from BEVERLOO Camp,
these consisted chiefly of 1917 class recruits and a small proportion
of "returned wounded" men. These reinforcements belonged to various
regiments, but the larger proportion were trained at the depots of the
2nd Foot Guards, 161st and 262nd Inf.Regts.

Method of Holding the Line.   The main line of defence is now the
                              "DALEVAL Line", the sector of the 262nd
Inf.Regt. being held by 3 Coys. The old German front line is only
held by posts, each company in front line providing 1 N.C.O. and 6 men
at night and during the day time 1 N.C.O. and 3 men for this purpose.
Posts are relieved every 12 hours. There is also a chain of double
sentry posts in each company sector at intervals of about 200 yards,
between the "Old German Line" and the DALEVAL Line, in the prisoner's
Coy sector this chain of sentry posts is along DORA trench. The 4th
Coy of the Battn. in front line and a whole Battn. of the 262nd Res.
Regt are said to be in reserve at AUBERS. The old Battn. of the
regiment is in rest billets at SANTES.

DALEVAL Line.   In the prisoner's company sector (S. of the
                FAUQUISSART Road) this line consists of breastworks. It
is not in a very advanced stage of completion, in many places the
parados is lacking. The garrison is accomodated in concrete dug-outs,
mostly situated in houses, close behind or in front of the DALEVAL line;
there are very few concrete dug-outs in the DALEVAL line itself. The
trenches are well revetted and are quite dry. Wiring parties are out
every night working in front of the new DALEVAL line.

    Their orders are to hold front line posts against any local
action on our part, but, if an attack is carried out, to fall back to
the DALEVAL line which is to be held as long as possible.

Machine Guns.   None of the light pattern machine guns have yet been
                issued, although during the VIMY fighting some of the
regiments of the 79th Res. Div. were supplied with them, but were withdrawn again when the Division left the VIMY area.

    The 262nd Res. Inf. Regt. lost about half its machine guns during
the battle, either destroyed or captured. At present there are about

                                                           (Continued)

(continued)

16 - 18 machine guns in the regiment.

Trench Mortars. Prisoner thinks for the moment that there is shortage of trained men for firing T.Ms. A trench mortar school has been started in SANTES.

Gas. No gas cylinders have been seen by prisoners in this sector.

Casualties. The 202nd Res. Inf. Regt. suffered very heavy casualties during the battle. The 7th Coy went in 180 strong and came out with 14 men, the 5th Coy also went in with about 180 men and came out with 4 men. The losses in officers were also very severe, losing at least two-thirds of their establishment.

Artillery. The artillery of the 79th Res. Div. is already in line. The prisoner states their D.A.C. lost a large number of horses during the battle, owing to our accurate artillery fire on their communications.

Rest Billets. The resting battn. of 202nd. Res. Inf. Regt. is billetted in the laundry in V.E.D., S.E. of SANTES.

Reliefs. 202nd Res. Inf. Regt. relieved 5th Bav. Regt. on night of 4/5th. Relief started from SANTES at 9 p.m. and was complete shortly after midnight. Small advanced parties were sent forward a day or two before to act as guides.

Commanding Officers.   79th Res. Division   =   General de Infanterie von BACKMEISTER.
                       202nd Res. Inf.Regt. =   Oberstlt. ROTENHAHN.
                       II Battn.   -do-   =   Hauptmann KAISER.
                         -do-   Adjt.   =   Lt.MULLER.
                         -do-   7th Coy. = Lt.TRENN.

Headquarters. Company H.Q. in DELEVAL Line is a strong concrete dig-out.

Rations. Field kitchens are in AUBERS. Carrying parties bring food into trenches between 9 and 10 in the evening, and 3 and 4 in the morning. Prisoner does not know what time rations arrive at AUBERS.

General. RUSSIAN prisoners are working on the trenches at SANTES, constructing concrete dug-outs.
He had heard there is a long range gun at SANTES, but does not know its position.
During the battle the Div.H.Q. of the 79th Res. Div. was at DROCOURT and then moved back to DOURGES.
The morale of the troops, especially that of the newly arrived drafts, is very bad, and their physique is also poor.

Vol 22

22C
16 sheets

SECRET.

WAR DIARY.

OF

1/8th Batt. West York Regt.

FOR

June 1917.

Army Form C. 2118.

WAR DIARY
INTELLIGENCE SUMMARY
(Erase heading not required.)

1/8 WEST YORKSHIRE REGT

Place	Date	Hour	Summary of Events and Information	Remarks and references to Appendices
LAVENTIE	1·6·17	—	Total strength of Battalion 32 Officers 890 O.R. Ration " " 24 " 738 " 2nd Lt A.L. FELL left for England in connection with his application for a commission in the INDIAN ARMY	MAP REFS AUBERS 36SW 1 & 1/10000
do	2·6·17	—	Lt. Col. R.A. HUDSON D.S.O. returned from 146 Infantry Brigade and resumed command of the Battalion. MAJOR T. LONGBOTTOM resumed command of "C" Company. Capt. H.R. LUPTON MC and 2nd Lt A.M. RAMSDEN returned from Leave. A Church Parade service was held at 9 am.	
do	3·6·17	—	The undernamed W.O. and N.C.O. of the unit are mentioned in Sir DOUGLAS HAIG's dispatch of 9·4·17, submitting names deserving of special mention:— 305009 A/RSM WELDON (T 305/66 L/Cpl DUNN) F.W. Authority — Supplement to London Gazette 21/22·5·17	
do	4·6·17	—	The Battalion concluded 4 days training, while in billets in LAVENTIE the hours of training being 6.30-8 am and 9am to 1 pm. Special attention in was paid to Musketry attack practice, and Patrol formations. In addition the officers met for an hour in the afternoon under the Commanding Officer for Tactical and an NCOs Class for an hour under the R.S.M. for Drill and Musketry.	

2449 Wt. W14957/M90 750,000 1/16 J.B.C. & A. Forms/C.2118/12.

Army Form C. 2118.

WAR DIARY
or
INTELLIGENCE SUMMARY

(Erase heading not required.)

1/8 WEST YORKSHIRE REGT

Instructions regarding War Diaries and Intelligence Summaries are contained in F.S. Regs., Part II. and the Staff Manual respectively. Title Pages will be prepared in manuscript.

Place	Date	Hour	Summary of Events and Information	Remarks and references to Appendices
LAVENTIE and TRENCHES M34c55.17 to N13c40.58	5.6.17	—	The Battalion relieved the 1/4 WEST YORKSHIRE REGT in the trenches. A Co on the Right, D Co. Centre, C Co Left. B Co in support. The relief commenced from LAVENTIE at 8 pm and was completed by 10.30 pm without incident.	
do	6.6.17	—	10 Large booby-trap grenades left in LAVENTIE under a guard post in the vicinity of the Dump for the purpose of being trained cautiously in the use of them. Platoons and companies. 2/Lt A.L. MORTIMER and 5 O.R. proceeded to ENGLAND on leave. A fighting patrol of 1 officer (2/Lt RAMSDEN A Co) and 32 OR left our lines on the right and crossed to enemy front line at M.24.d.42.06 getting to N.30.b.6.1. No sign of the enemy was seen in the enemy's lines. Heavy enemy trench & Grenade fire opened up on our wire. 2 hours the patrol returned to our lines.	
do	7.6.17	—	The trial of 306462 Rfn. J.H. FARNELL of A Co. by F.G.C.M. took place at H.Q. 146 Infantry Brigade the charge being "Deserting His Majesty's Service." Major BRAITHWAITE M.C. 1/7 W.Y.R. being President, 2/Lt AMILIGAN, Prosecutor, Calls 2/Lt A.M. RAMSDEN, officer in charge of the half of the accused. Rfn FARNELL was found guilty, and sentenced to 20 years penal servitude. At 11.5 pm the 1/7 WEST YORKSHIRE REGT carried out a raid on the enemy trenches. No enemy were encountered and the raiding party suffered no casualties.	

2449 Wt. W14957/M90 750,000 1/16 J.B.C. & A. Forms/C.2118/12.

Army Form C. 2118.

WAR DIARY
INTELLIGENCE SUMMARY

(Erase heading not required.)

1/8 WEST YORKSHIRE REGT

Place	Date	Hour	Summary of Events and Information	Remarks and references to Appendices
TRENCHES M2LC55.17 to N13C40.58	8.6.17	—	Continued reconnaissance of the enemy's front and support lines in enemy's territory during the night to ascertain the enemy war forms on the front of the trench of our battalion.	
do	9.6.17	—	The battalion was relieved in the trenches by the 1/7 WEST YORKSHIRE REGT and proceeded to billets in LAVENTIE, with Battalion Headquarters at COCKSHY HOUSE. During the afternoon all men of the battalion were bathed.	
do LAVENTIE	10.6.17	—	The battalion relieved the 1/6 WEST YORKSHIRE REGT in the posts on the RUE DU BACQUEROT. At night working parties of 3 officers and 136 O.R. were supplied. 2ND LT A.L. BAKER left for ENGLAND on leave.	
SUPPORT (HQ M14 C 3.1)	11.6.17	—	Working parties of 4 officers and 186 O.R. were furnished during the day. Men not so engaged in working parties carried on with Musketry, Patrol formations &c and practice in trench digging and rapid wiring.	
do	12.6.17	—	Capt. W.H. BROOKE M.C. returned to the unit from 146 Infantry Brigade and resumed the duties of Adjutant. do. 2ND LT W.C. KEMP rejoined HQ military crops for gallantry and devotion to duty.	

WAR DIARY or INTELLIGENCE SUMMARY

Army Form C. 2118.

Place	Date	Hour	Summary of Events and Information	Remarks and references to Appendices
SUPPORT TRENCHES (H.Q. Mid 2.1) M34e55.17 to N13c40.58 do	13.6.17	—	The Battalion Relieved the 1/4 West Yorkshire Regt in the trenches in the right subsector. D.Co. on the Right, C.Co. Centre, A.Co. left, B.Co. Support. At night they were patrolling & was carried out, the enemy wire from S to be holding their trenches by means of posts.	
	14.6.17	—	The 1/6 West Riding Regt. Relieved our company that are in the trenches by the Battalion from M24e55.17 to M24d67.82. This unit furnished to the left and took over the trenches from M24.67.82 to N14.a17.30. Our Disposition were as follows. D.Co. Right, C.Co. Centre, A.Co. Left, B.Co. in Syphon. During the night patrols were out all night from the Company Coln: by front line. They reported that the enemy wire was being held in much greater force than at had been the case for sometime past. Battle Coy. supplied the loss of 2 men — 1 killed and 1 missing	
	15.6.17		The Battalion moved back into the trenches on the Right Subsector from M24.d.55.17 to N13c40.58. The 1/6 West Riding Regt moving out	
	16.6.17		2 NO 17 W.H. PORRITT left for X1 Corps Sniping School Bourz " A SEYMOUR left for 1/46 Inf Brigade University Course. " A.L. MORTIMER returned from Our leave.	

WAR DIARY

or INTELLIGENCE SUMMARY

1/8 WEST YORKSHIRE REGT

Army Form C. 2118.

Place	Date	Hour	Summary of Events and Information	Remarks and references to Appendices
TRENCHES M24c55.17 to N13c40.SE	16.6.17		During the night a patrol from the 6th Co (OC) reconnoitred the TRAVERSE. The ground was found to be much cut up. No enemy were encountered.	
	17.6.17		The Battalion was relieved in the trenches by the 1/7 WEST YORKSHIRE Regt and proceeded to billets in LAVENTIE.	See Appendix A
LOYS LAVENTIE	18.6.17		The companies carried on with Battalion Training.	
ROAD	19.6.17		Training was carried out.	
WOOD	20.6.17		Continued training, with special reference to taking posts in enemy line.	
WOOD	21.6.17		The Battalion stood down [at] 5.30 a.m. owing to the relief was postponed.	
WOOD	22.6.17		Continued with training. The operation of Taking posts being again postponed.	
WOOD	23.6.17		The Battn relieved the 1/7 W.Y. on the night subwater, on the right were the 1/5 Aus. on the right the 1/5 Regt P.E.T. The relief was without incident.	
TEMPLE BAR TRENCHES	24.6.17 to 28.6.17		It very quiet tour. No casualties. The Battalion was very active with patrols on the whole front sending a considerable time each night in the German front and support lines. Its enemy trench mortars were successfully brought to bear on enemy working parties.	See Appendix B
	29.6.17		The Battn. was relieved by the 1/7 Dof y Lanc Regt, without incident and moved into Brigade Support, with H.Q. at RED HOUSE. 2/Lt Currie reported back from 1st Army School	See Appendix C
TEMPLE BAR	30.6.17		The Battn provided working parties which took up all available men, after finishing first garrisons. Casualties during month OFFICERS NIL. O.R. Killed -- 2 Wounded -- 5 Missing -- 1	

Strength at end of June OFFICERS 30 O.R. 873

"A"

OPERATION ORDERS NO. 52

By LIEUT-COL.R.A.HUDSON, D.S.O. - Commanding:-1/8th.West Yorkshire Regt.

June 16th.1917.

Reference Map - AUBERS. 36. S.W. 1. 1/10.000.

RELIEF.

The Battalion will be relieved in the trenches to-morrow 17/6/17 by the 1/7th.Bn.West Yorkshire Regiment.
Relief will commence about 10.30.a.m.
On relief the Battalion will move to Billets in LAVENTIE, and will be met outside the Town by the respective C.Q.M.Sgts.

ROUTES.

A. and B. Coys.　　　　　- Via FME EPINETTE, LA FLINQUE.

C. " D. " & H.Q.　- " RED HOUSE.

TRANSPORT.

1 Limber per Company will be provided to-morrow to carry the Lewis Guns, Ammunition, and Mess Stores.

Limbers will be at M.23.a.0.6. for A. and B. Coys. and at Junction of RUE MASSELOT & RUE BACQUEROT for C. and D. Coys. at 11.0.a.m.

The Mess Cart will be at H.Q. at 11.0.a.m.

GENERAL.

(a) A. Company will be on duty on arrival in LAVENTIE, and will provide the Orderly Officer.

(b) A. Company will also detail a Regimental Guard of 1 Sergeant, 1 Corporal and 7 men to report to the R.S.M. at Headquarters as soon as possible after arrival.

(c) Completion of relief in the trenches will be reported in B.A.B.

(d) Companies will notify H.Q. as soon as they are in Billets in LAVENTIE.

Captain,
Adjutant. 1/8th.Bn.West Yorkshire Regiment.

SECRET.

OPERATION ORDERS NO. 33.

By LIEUT-COL.R.A.HUDSON, D.S.O. - Commanding.1/8th.West Yorkshire Regt.

Reference Map - AUBERS. 36. S.W. 1. 1/10.000.

1. **RELIEF.**

    The Battalion will relieve the 1/7th.West Yorkshire Regiment in the trenches in the Right Sub-sector to-morrow 23/6/17.

'A' Company.	---	On the Right.
'B' "	---	Centre.
'C' "	---	On the Left.
'D' "	---	Support.

2. **ORDER OF RELIEF & TIMES.**

    1st Platoon of 'A' Company will move at 9- 0.a.m.
    1st   "   of 'B'   "   "   " at 9-20.a.m.
    1st   "   of 'C'   "   "   " at 9- 0.a.m.
    1st   "   of 'D'   "   "   " at 9-20.a.m.
    H.Q. will move at 10-15.a.m.

3. **ROUTES.**

    A. and B. Coys.   Via FORT D'ESQUIN, LA FLINQUE & FME EPINETTE
    C. " D. "   " RED HOUSE.
    Headquarters.   " -do-

    Guides will not be provided.

4. **TRANSPORT.**

    1 Limber per Company will be provided, and will move 5 minutes ahead of the respective Companies.

    Limbers for A. and B. Coys to M.23.a.0.6.
    "   "   C. " D. "   to Junction of RUE MASSELOT & RUE
                                                    (BACQUEROT.
    The Mess Cart will be at H.Q. at 10.0.a.m. and the M.O.Cart at the AID POST at the same time.

5. **GENERAL.**

    (a) 1 Officer per Coy, C.S.M, Coy. & H.Q.Gas N.C.O's will proceed one hour in advance to take over details of work, stores, and gas appliances respectively.
    (b) A return of Ammunition & Stores taken over by this Unit in the trenches, will be rendered to Orderly Room by 5 p.m. 23/6/17.
    (c) Coys will make their own arrangements for handing in to the Q.M.Stores, Officers Kits and Surplus Mess Stores.
    (d) Completion of relief will be reported by the code word "THIRD".

June 22nd.1917.

(Sgd) W. H. B R O O K E,
Captain,
Adjutant. 1/8th.Bn.West Yorkshire Regt.

SECRET   **OPERATION ORDERS NO. 33.**

By LIEUT-COL. R.A.HUDSON, D.S.O.- Comdg. 1/8th.Bn.West Yorkshire Regt.

Reference Map - AUBERS. 36. S.W. 1. 1/10,000.

1. RELIEF.

The Battalion will be relieved in the trenches to-morrow 29/6/17, by the 1/7th.Bn.West Yorkshire Regiment.
On relief the Battalion will move into Support in the RUE BACQUEROT Line as follows:-

'A' Company.	---	ROAD BEND POST.
'B' "	---	DEAD END & PICANTIN POSTS.
'C' "	---	HOUGOUMONT, MASSELOT & APPLE HOUSE.
'D' "	---	WANGERIE & LONELY POSTS.

Relief will commence about 9-30.a.m.

2. TRANSPORT.

1 Limber will be provided to carry the surplus Lewis Gun Ammunition from TEMPLE BAR to RED HOUSE, and will be at TEMPLE BAR at 9.0.a.m.

The Mess Cart and the M.O.Cart will be provided by the 1/7th.West Yorkshire Regiment.

3. GENERAL.

(a) 1 Officer per Company, and 1 N.C.O. and 2 men for each Post will proceed in advance and take over from the 1/7th.West Yorkshire Regiment. The Officer will report to the Company H.Q. concerned, and the N.C.O. and 2 men will report direct to the Post they are taking over by 8-30.a.m.

(b) The Company at DEAD END POST will detail 1 man to take over from the 1/7th.West Yorkshire R. at HARLECH CASTLE, by 8-30.a.m.

(c) Only to-morrow's breakfast rations will be brought up to-night, the remainder of to-morrow's rations will be brought up to the Posts to-morrow.

(d) A return of Stores & Ammunition taken over will be rendered to Orderly Room by 4 p.m.

(e) Sick Parade to-morrow will be at RED HOUSE at 12 noon.

(f) Completion of relief will be reported to H.Q. by the Code word "NINTH".

1/8TH BATTALION.
WEST YORKS
REGIMENT.
No. 52/27
Date June 28th. 1917.

Captain,
Adjutant - 1/8th.Bn.West Yorkshire Regt.

SECRET.

WAR DIARY.

OF

1/8th Batt. West Yorks Reg.

FOR

July.

1917.

Army Form C. 2118.

WAR DIARY
INTELLIGENCE SUMMARY
(Erase heading not required.)

1/8 West Yorkshire Regt.

Place	Date	Hour	Summary of Events and Information	Remarks and references to Appendices
RED HOUSE M.B.D.2.1. RUGERS 36WF	July 1		The Battalion remained in support at RED HOUSE. Move training was undertaken in HARBOCH CASTLE area as the working parties were reduced.	
	2		Continued training & providing working parties	
	3		The Battn. "stood to" for a raid during the morning but did not have to move	
	4		Major Sykes M.C. deferred to England and senior officers, Major Houghton assuming the duties of C. in C. in Command. A/Lt. Hudson went on leave	
	5		The Battalion relieved the 1/7 Battn in trenches, leaving the 1/5 W.Y. Rs on the right & the 1/2 P.P. army (?)	
TEMPLE BAR	6			
	7			
	8		A quiet time in trenches, working to refit	
	9		The Battalion was relieved by the 12th Regt. P.E.F. & moved to LE NOUVEAU MONDE	
LE NOUVEAU MONDE	10			
	11		The Battalion remained in billets and trained during the morning and made	
	12		preparation for moving. 2/Lt NETTLETON rejoined from duty in England. A quiet time, nothing of interest to record	
	13		The Battalion less A Co. entrained at LESTREM and proceeded to new area at Fort MARDICK (near DUNKIRK) arriving in camp at 7am. The journey was completed without incident. A Co. entrained at LESTREM on the morning of the 14th & joined the Battalion the same day	
FORT MARDYCK	14		2nd Lt. BAKER returned from XI Corps Sniping School	
do	15		Parried on with training. 2/Lt CALLAGHAN proceeded on leave	
do	16		2/Lt. MILLIGAN left for 1st Army School. The Battalion left FORT MARDYCK and proceeded by march route to new area at ZUYDE COOTE	
ZUYDECOOTE	17		The Battalion left ZUYDECOOTE and moved by march route to COXYDE. The move	
COXYDE	18		was completed without incident. Lt Col F. WILKINSON M.C. returned from leave	

Lt Col F. WILKINSON M.C.

2449 Wt. W14957/M90 750,000 1/16 J.B.C. & A. Forms/C.2118/12.

Army Form C. 2118.

WAR DIARY
or
INTELLIGENCE SUMMARY

(Erase heading not required.)

1/8 WEST YORKSHIRE REG^T

Place	Date	Hour	Summary of Events and Information	Remarks and references to Appendices
COXYDE	1917 July 18		The battalion moved by march route to NIEUPORT to support relieving the 16th Battⁿ NORTHUMBERLAND FUSILIERS. The line – St GEORGES Sector was held by the 1/6 WEST YORKSHIRE REG^T on the right and the 1/5 W.Y.R. on the left.	
NIEUPORT	19		Lt Col R.A. HUDSON D.S.O. returned from leave and assumed command of the Battalion.	
	20		The battalion continued in support. NIEUPORT was shelled almost continuously and it was difficult to move about. Working parties were furnished nightly.	
	21		On the night of the 21/22nd NIEUPORT was subjected to severe bombardments of gas shells mixed with H.E. These bombardments took place at 9 p.m. and 11 p.m. when 21st and against 2 a.m. in the 22nd each bombardment lasting for half an hour. The guns used about 3 miles (4700 yards) and total for gas shells on each occasion was shells mixed with H.E. then causing the gas shell to be mistaken for duds in the first bombardment after the bombardment the effect of the gas seemed very slight. About enough many men became sick and stayed vomiting and undoubtedly many crouched in cause their too respirators on soundly and were regarded owing, not keep by the mixture of H.E. with the gas shell. He thinks being mistaken for	

WAR DIARY or INTELLIGENCE SUMMARY

Army Form C. 2118.

1/8 West Yorkshire Regt

Place	Date	Hour	Summary of Events and Information	Remarks and references to Appendices
NIEUPORT	1917 July 21		"Ypres" and by the smell being unfamiliar. The main symptoms are influence upon the eye, and conjunctivitis vomiting of the sea sickness type, sometimes Diarrhoea, and abdominal pain, skin Erythema, Catarrh it may form that Bronchitis develops in a number of cases leading in some instances to Broncho-pneumonia. The shells appear to have been of the 77m type with single copper driving bands, shoulder painted a drab yellow, long pointed blunt with a small drab cross. The smell of the gas was that of mustard and slightly of garlic. When I am on the 22nd the men's eyes became so affected that blindness ??? Cameron every ??? officer and man with the battalion in NIEUPORT was affected, and with the exception of 4 officers and 40 men had to be sent to hospital on the 22nd. The total casualties of the battalion up to the night of the	

Army Form C. 2118.

WAR DIARY
or
INTELLIGENCE SUMMARY
(Erase heading not required.)

1/7 WEST YORKSHIRE REGT

Place	Date	Hour	Summary of Events and Information	Remarks and references to Appendices
NIEUPORT	1917 July 22		22/7/17 Strength 18 officers and 662 other ranks. The following is a list of the officers:— Lt. Col R.A. Hudson DSO, Major T. Longbottom, Major W.H. Brooke MC, Capt E. Billington, Capt H.R. Lupton MC, Capt E.R. Wilkinson MC, Lt S. Bellhouse, Lt A.M. Ramsden, 2nd Lts D.I. Currie W.H. Pirritt, S.N. Hughes, C.E. Shelly, E.N. Firth, A. Seymour, A.L. Mortimer, S.N. Weaver, W.E. Worsley and Capt L. Meakin RAMC at duty. Lt W.G. Kemp, 2nd Lt T. Nettleton, H.L. Baker and H. Lennox. The following officers were also slightly affected by continued MAJOR BROOKE MC took over command of the battalion in Lt Col Hudson OBO, being sent to hospital. At night the battalion was relieved from Nieuport and proceeded	
NIEUPORT (BELGIUM SHEET 11SE)	23		to R.F. Baillet Camp, near Oost-Dunkerke. LT W.G. KEMP took over temporary command of the battalion vice Major Brooke MC, who returned to hospital from effects of gas.	
	24		22/16. Capt J.E. Appleyard proceeded on special leave of 14 days to England. 2nd Lt J.H. Turner returned from leave. Major W.H. Braithwaite MC. 1/7 West Yorkshire Regt arrived and assumed temporary command of the battalion a further 79 OR who have been in the gas shell barrage on 22nd June	

2449 Wt. W14957/M90 750,000 1/16 J.B.C. & A. Forms/C.2118/12.

WAR DIARY

INTELLIGENCE SUMMARY

Army Form C. 2118.

1/8 WEST YORKSHIRE REGT.

Place	Date	Hour	Summary of Events and Information	Remarks and references to Appendices
COST-DUNKERQUE	1917 Aug 24		to hospital. 2nd Lt S. ILLINGWORTH proceeded to 49 Div. HQ to assume Traffic Control duties under A.P.M.	
R.I.BAILLET CAMP R.3rd (BELGIUM SHEET 11 SE)	25		2nd Lts R.W. HORSFALL and H. NORTHROP joins the battalion.	
	26		Lt & Q.M. B. FARRAR proceeds on leave. 2nd Lt W.S. ROTHERA returns to the battalion from leave.	
	27		During the shelling of our battery positions near the camp 2nd Lt H.R.P. WRIGHT and Capt ROBILLARD (RAMC) were slightly wounded and proceeded to hospital.	
	28		Capt H. DIXON 1/6 D of W (WEST RIDING) REGT joined the battalion and assumed the duties of second in command. During the night of the 28/29th the vicinity of the camp was shelled with the new gas shells. Box respirators were worn for about 4 hours. No casualties occurred.	
	29		2nd Lt L.W. CALLAGHAN returned from leave. 2nd Lt A. MILLIGAN recalled from First Army School, reported.	
	30		The battalion cadre assumes the duties of Advance.	
	31		Nothing of importance occurred.	

Army Form C. 2118.

WAR DIARY
INTELLIGENCE SUMMARY

(Erase heading not required.)

1/8 WEST YORKSHIRE REGT.

Place	Date	Hour	Summary of Events and Information	Remarks and references to Appendices
RIBAILLET CAMP. R.35.d. (BELGIUM Sheet 11SE)	1917 July 31		Owing to the small number of men with the Battalion (about 25) after providing for transport, QM Stores, and Battalion duties) no organized training could be carried on the 31st and 31/7/17 a working party of 11 OR was provided. The remainder of the men were casualties in musketry, PD & BF and Drill. Since arrival in camp the men have been carried out under considerable difficulty, owing the intense activity of the enemy batteries of artillery surrounding the camp. Total casualties for the month are as follows.	

```
                                Officers    O.R
Killed in action                    —        1
Died of wounds                      —        1
Wounds-till live                    —        2
Wounded-remained on duty            —        1
Wounded- Shell Gas                  —       18
    do        do  remained on duty  —        4
                                         ————
                                   Battalion Strength Total   14    246
                                              Ration          11    146
```

741 (details) 6
40 (Casualties forms) 31-7-17

"SECRET".

WAR DIARY.

OF

18th Batt West Yorks Regt

FOR

August 1917

Army Form C. 2118.

WAR DIARY
INTELLIGENCE SUMMARY
(Erase heading not required.)

1/8 WEST YORKSHIRE REGT

Place	Date	Hour	Summary of Events and Information	Remarks and references to Appendices
RABAILLET CAMP Nr COXYDE	1917 Aug 1		The Battalion was relieved by the 16th Northumberland Fusiliers and proceeded to tents near Coxyde. The relief was completed without incident.	
COXYDE	2		Battalion was relieved at 4.30 pm by a battalion of the H.L.I. and proceeded to Ghyvelde arriving at 8.30 pm. Capt C.J.C. La Coste MC joins the Battalion	
GHYVELDE D.21.C. (Sheet 19 BELGIUM & FRANCE)	3		The Battalion moved again by march route to billets near Teteghem. All men in the Battalion with exception of Transport, QM Stores, personnel were formed into a composite company under the command of Lieut W.G. Kemp M.C.	
	4		A party of 4 officers and 169 ohs. march joined the unit. The officers being 2nd Lts S.W. Allen, F.H. Watkin, G. Rhys and J.S.G. Dorn. The men were split up into three parties, one third going each to A, B and C Companies.	
	5		The organization of the battalion then was three Companies of two Platoons each, and one section of D Co attached to B Co. The Companies were commanded as follows:- A Co. Capt C.J.C. La Coste MC B Co. Lt W.G. Kemp MC C Co. 2nd Lt W. Callaghan. A draft of 31 other ranks arrived and were distributed in the proportion of 7/13 to each Company.	

Army Form C. 2118.

WAR DIARY
INTELLIGENCE SUMMARY
(Erase heading not required.)

1/8 WEST YORKSHIRE REGT

Place	Date	Hour	Summary of Events and Information	Remarks and references to Appendices
ETEGHEM	1917 Aug 5	—	The ordinary training of the Battalion was resumed. Two Lewis Gun sections needed to be trained in their own arm, 1 Officer and 12 men were sent to the Brigade school for signalling and Stretcher Bearer classes takes under the M.O.	
	6		19 O.R. (including the R.S.M.) admitted to hospital from the effects of gas. 2 warrant officers also joined the Battalion. 2nd Lts W H Backhouse, J Hudson, A E Rolls, and W E Glasgow. Capt T E Amyot (RAMC) also joined the Battalion, and took up his duties as Medical Officer.	
	7			
	8		2nd Lt H Lennox proceeded to England on leave. The Corps Commander XV Corps (Lt Gen Sir J P Du Cane, K.C.B) inspects the Battalion on the training area.	
	9 10		The Battalion continued with the usual training which during this week was carried out on the Dunes, about 2 hours march from billets, and in consequence of this only two hours actual training on the ground was done.	
	12		The Mc Cron had Church parade in the morning followed by a Tactical scheme for Officers. The Battalion moves to Bomb at after the Church parade (when the Battalion moves to Bomb at	

Army Form C. 2118.

WAR DIARY
or
INTELLIGENCE SUMMARY
(Erase heading not required.)

1/8 West Yorkshire Regt

Instructions regarding War Diaries and Intelligence Summaries are contained in F.S. Regs, Part II. and the Staff Manual respectively. Title Pages will be prepared in manuscript.

Place	Date	Hour	Summary of Events and Information	Remarks and references to Appendices
Fort de Dunes C16a (Sheet 19 Belgium and France)	1917 Aug 12/13	—	Fort de Dunes (C16a Sheet 19 Belgium and France) 2nd Lt W.A. Dedman proceeded to England on leave.	
	15		2nd Lt J.S.C. Dorn was attached to 146 Trench Mortar Battery for duty.	
	16		2nd Lts W. Rennyard and J.E. Featherstone joined the unit.	
	17		2nd Lts J. Buckley and W. Metcalfe joined the unit.	
	18		2nd Lt F.T.H. Watkin proceeded to England on leave. During the week nothing the state of progress was made in training the platoons composing the Battalion. A draft of 231 Other ranks arrived and were distributed to Companies as follows:— A.Co. 43 B.Co. 44 C.Co. 49 D.Co. 95 each. Each Platoon was then organised & 4 companies of 4 platoons bombing sections being made up to full strength.	
	19			
	20		2Lt D.N. Seannie A.S.C. joined the unit.	
	22		The G.O.C. Division inspected the transport of the Battalion and expressed himself as being well pleased with the turnout.	

WAR DIARY or INTELLIGENCE SUMMARY

Army Form C. 2118.

1/8 WEST YORKSHIRE REGT

Place	Date	Hour	Summary of Events and Information	Remarks and references to Appendices
FORT DE DUNES C.16.a (Sheet 19 BELGIUM and FRANCE)	1917 Aug 22	—	A draft of 26 other Ranks arrived and were posted in equal proportions to the different Companies. 2nd Lt B.J. RICHARDSON joined the unit.	
	24		Capt M.H.R. LUPTON MC rejoined the unit and assumed command of D Co.	
	25		A draft of 27 other ranks joined the unit. Major W.H. BROOKE M.C. rejoined the unit. During the week a further progress was made in training. Bombing and Lewis Gun instruction was given particularly attention and training of recruits and runners continued. Several practice trench to trench attacks by Companies were carried out as well as a Battalion practice attack. The hours of training were from 8.30 to 1 p.m. and in addition Officers N.C.Os and men did P.T. Lewis 0.20 in the afternoon doing tactical schemes, N.C.Os. under the R.S.M.	
	26		Lt. Col. R.A. HUDSON DSO rejoined the unit and assumed command	
	27		Training was carried on as usual. A new Specialbomb Class of 12 men was formed.	

Army Form C. 2118.

WAR DIARY
INTELLIGENCE SUMMARY
(Erase heading not required.)

1/8 WEST YORKSHIRE REGT

Instructions regarding War Diaries and Intelligence Summaries are contained in F.S. Regs., Part II. and the Staff Manual respectively. Title Pages will be prepared in manuscript.

Place	Date	Hour	Summary of Events and Information	Remarks and references to Appendices
FORT. DE DUNES. C.16.a.	1917 Aug 28		The Battalion moved by march route from the camp at Fort de Dunes to billets in GHYVELDE, arriving at the latter place at 11.30 am. A heavy gale was blowing considerably hampering the men on the march.	
GHYVELDE D.21.b. (sheet 19) (Belgium & France)	29		A draft of 33 other ranks joined the Battalion, with the exception of one man they were all men who had been gassed on the 21/22 July. 2nd Lt C.J.B. SMITH A.S.C. joined the Battalion. MAJOR W.H. BRAITHWAITE M.C. (rejoined) 1/7 W.Y.R. and Capt. HUDSON D.S.O. assuming command. Lt E.C. DUDGEON and 2nd Lt.	
	30		Training was hampered by rehuis stormy weather. Training was carried on anyway. Lt G.E. GREEN (A.S.C.) joined the unit, also a draft of 29 other ranks. 2nd Lieuts. R.O. BOWRAN	
	31		The following officers joined the unit:- 2nd Lieuts. R.O. BOWRAN, W. GARDNER, E. SMITH, T. BAIRSTOW, W.C. KITCHING, C.C. STUDLEY, H.G. LOVER. The usual training was carried out on the training area. Special attention was being paid at this time to close and extended order drill, musketry, bombing and wire cutting at the training of Lewis Gunners and	

Army Form C. 211

WAR DIARY
or
INTELLIGENCE SUMMARY

(Erase heading not required.)

1/8 WEST YORKSHIRE REGT

Place	Date	Hour	Summary of Events and Information	Remarks references to Appendices

CHYNELO BOIS
021.6
(Sheet 19)
BELGFRANCE
	1917
	Aug 31
			Other officers to -
			Strength of the Battalion:-
			         1st Aug 1917 31st Aug 1917
			       Officers O.R. Officers O.R.
			Total strength 15 243 43 817
			Ration 14 157 33 737
			
			Casualties for August 1917
			            Officers O.R.
			Occupancy with unit during month — 1
			Reported dying in Hospital
			(previously struck off the strength
			as wounded - Gas) — 87
			Transferred to England (previously
			reported wounded - Gas 11 426
			Rejoined from Hospital - Gas 3 54
			Reinforcements 27 519	

Officer comdg West Yorks Regt
1/8 West Yorkshire Regt

War Diary
Vol 25
of
14th Batt. West Yorks Regt
for
September 1917

25C.
4 sheets

WAR DIARY or INTELLIGENCE SUMMARY

Army Form C. 2118.

Place	Date	Hour	Summary of Events and Information	Remarks and references to Appendices
			[see war diary appx]	
	16		From the 2nd & 3rd till the 23rd the Battn remained in cmd of 6/7/12.05 Training of all ranks was carried on including a number of Brigade & Divl Schemes. The training was	
	23rd		carried out during excellent weather. The Battn had the honor of the Bn being visited by H.M. The King on 21st Sept to accept 30 Officers and men from various units of Regular Bns of the RASC men from MALTA and men from various depots of Regular Bns of the RASC men from MALTA were regrouped by 2nd Lt. Falwihpuk from Major of the 5th & attached the duties of 2/Lt Major hergettern repoured the 2/Lt with Bingham of Major Brown 1/6 W.R.R. left the earlier the 17th Revs, removed to assist on 2.2.1.16 3 O.R. renewed in the 4.2 O.R the Bingham were expelled as raring inferior	
			10th 3/R Heard 6 2/Lt Callaghan 2/Lt DAWN & 100 Joined	
	17th		Major ESACHE joined & resumed the duties of 2nd 1/c	
	18th		2/Lt Smith was transferred to 18th W.Y. Rt	
	20th		Lt Cmdt. To 19 O.R. arrived. 1 on the 22nd	
	21st		The Battn moved by march routes to TEREGEM	
	24th		" " " " " WORMHOUDT	
	25th		" " " " " NOORDPEENE. 2/Lt aus and 18 minutes	
	26th		Commissioned services were furnished total badges to march to Prentmsmd	
	27th		On Training to O.R. jumad	

Army Form C. 2118.

WAR DIARY
or
INTELLIGENCE SUMMARY

(Erase heading not required.)

Place	Date	Hour	Summary of Events and Information	Remarks and references to Appendices
NOORDPEENE TATINGHEM	29th 30th		The Battn. moved by march route to TATINGHEM. The Division practised two Brigades in the attack. 2nd Battn. marched to [illegible]. Total strength at end of Sept. Officers 47 O.R. 972	1/5 West Yorkshire Rt. R. Nelleson rejoined. P. M. Ardeen Lt Col. Comdg 1/5 W.Y. Rt.

SECRET.

WAR DIARY.

OF

1/2 Bn Australian Light Horse Rgt

FOR

1st to 31st October 1917

Army Form C. 2118.

WAR DIARY
or
INTELLIGENCE SUMMARY.
(Erase heading not required.)

1/8 West Yorkshire Regt

Place	Date	Hour	Summary of Events and Information	Remarks and references to Appendices
TATINGHEM	Oct 1st		The Battalion moved by march route to OXELAERE with HQ at a farm at D.29.b.6.8.	See Appendix A
	2nd		Training was carried out in attack formations & manoeuvres	
O.29.b.6.8	3rd		The Battn moved to WATOU area by march route via HQ at L.8.D.	See Appendix A(2) B(1)
L.8.D.	4th		Range Practices, Physical Training, musketry & attack practices & misc'l work	
L.8.D.	5th		The day was employed in preparing for action & all officers N.C.O. not going in with the Battn went to the Rear personnel camp or Rest Station or Transport lines	
L.8.D.	6th		The Battn entrained and moved into camp near VLAMERTINGHE	See Appendix C
VLAMERTINGHE	7th		The day was occupied by final preparations for action	
VLAMERTINGHE	8th		The morning was taken up by moving to ST JEAN where dinners were taken & sandbags, bombs and other stores drawn. At 5 P.M. in heavy rain the Battn, being the 2nd in the Brigade moved off to the Assembly Position. This entailed a 12 hour march in single file along hurried guides & duly to the darkness, gas in the guides & halts the was company only arrived in assembly position for the attack ment of PASSCHENDAELE five minutes before ZERO. In spite of almost insuperable difficulties of weather conditions & ground the Battn advanced under the barrage behind the Yorkshires B&C companies were detailed for the front, A&D for the	See Appendix D

Army Form C. 2118.

WAR DIARY
or
INTELLIGENCE SUMMARY.
(Erase heading not required.)

1/5 West Yorkshire Regt.

Instructions regarding War Diaries and Intelligence Summaries are contained in F. S. Regs., Part II. and the Staff Manual respectively. Title pages will be prepared in manuscript.

Place	Date	Hour	Summary of Events and Information	Remarks and references to Appendices
	9th		Second Objective owing to high casualties amongst Officers & NCOs the position became however much hostile machine gun fire & sniping was encountered & eventually the Battn dug itself in about 2/3 of its first objective after an advance of about 200 yards. H.Q. were established at KRONPRINZ FARM. The commanding officer Lt. Col. R.A. Hudson D.S.O. was killed early in the attack & the command devolved upon Major Brook M.C. the adjutant, who at one time had only two other officers besides himself available. Out of the 23 (nineteen?) officers who went in to with the unit eight were killed, eight were wounded, one missing & two wounded but remained at duty, this includes two London officers. 301 Casualties amongst O.R. On the night of the 10th inst.	See Appendix E
Attack on PASSCHENDAELE	10th		having been reinforced by a company of 1/4 W.R.R. YETH HOUSES was reached & held whilst the 5th NZRB got into position. Twelve on front were then withdrawn, relief being carried by Battn moved by	
	11th		march route to WELTJE where lorries were obtained & moved to rest & cleaned out four miles Culham Camp in the VLAMERTINGHE area.	
KAMERINGHE	12th		The Battn continued to rest and to WINNIEZEELE No 3 area.	See Appendix F

Army Form C. 2118.

WAR DIARY
or
INTELLIGENCE SUMMARY.
(Erase heading not required.)

1/8 West Yorkshire Regt.

Place	Date	Hour	Summary of Events and Information	Remarks and references to Appendices
WINNEZEELE	13		A quiet day employed in resting as the Battn. arrived at 11.30 pm the night before	
	14		As this was the first free day for some time every effort was made to clean & tidy kit	
	15		Training & baths	
	16		Training in assembling attack formations etc	
	17		Brigade commander's Parade. The Brigade was congratulated by G.O.C. II ANZAC Corps.	
	18		Training in formations of Battns and the G.O.C. drove round Brigade to say goodbye.	
	19"		Lt. Col. Remy (K.R.R.) D.S.O. took command of the Brigade.	
	20"		Training in musketry attack formations physical drill was carried out	
	21		Church Parades and Inspections.	
	22		Training on Range and wire continued	
	23		as for 22nd	
	24		as for 22nd	
	25		A fortnight's route march was carried out as training	
	26		The Battalion was inspected by the G.O.C. Brigade.	
	27		Training was continued.	
	28		The Battalion moved by march route to STEENVOORDE E. HQ. at 99.	Appendix G

Army Form C. 2118.

WAR DIARY
or
INTELLIGENCE SUMMARY.

(Erase heading not required.)

1/5 West Yorkshire Regt.

Place	Date	Hour	Summary of Events and Information	Remarks and references to Appendices
STEENVOORDE E.	29		The Battalion was occupied in clearing billets & route marches.	
	30		Training was continued in a.m. & windy weather. Coy Major and 1/1 Bn drawn & 101 O.R. reported	
	31		War spoon in No diary.	
			Casualties during month OFFICERS K O.R.K 46	See Appendix G
			W 7 W 166	
			D.O.W. 1 D.O.W. 6	
			M. 1 M 61	
			W. at duty 2 W at duty 15	
			Reinforcements during month OFFICERS 1 O.R. 117	
			Total strength at end of month OFFICERS 32 O.R. 769	

D. D. Dykes. Major
Comdg 1/5 West Yorkshire Regt.

Appendix A

SECRET.

146th INFANTRY BRIGADE OPERATION ORDER No. 73.

Ref. Map HAZEBROUCK Sheet 5a.   30th Sept. 1917.
and Sheet 27.

1. 146th Infantry Brigade Group will move to the ST MARIE CAPPEL area on the 1st October in accordance with attached table.

2. Distances to be maintained on the march:-

    100 yards between Companies and corresponding Units.

    500 yards between Battalions.

3. All halts will be at clock hour minus 10 minutes to clock hour. Long halt (1 hour, 10 minutes) from 12.50.p.m. to 2.0.p.m.

4. Brigade Office will be at Boys School, ST MARIE CAPPELLE.

5. ACKNOWLEDGE.

                 Fisher Captain,
         Brigade Major, 146th Infantry Brigade.

Issued at 5.0.p.m.

Copy No.	
1.	1/5th Bn. W. York. R.
2.	1/6th -do-
3.	1/7th -do-
4.	1/8th -do-
5.	146th Machine Gun Coy.
6.	146th Trench Mortar Battery.
7.	Staff Capt. 146th Brigade.
8.	O.C. No. 2 Signal Section.
9.	T.O. 146th Brigade.
10.	458th Field Coy. R.E.
11.	464th Coy. A.S.C.
12.	1/1st (W.R.) Field Amb.
13.	49th Division 'G'.
14.	-do- 'A' & 'Q'
15.	War Diary.
16.	Retained.
17.	"
18.	File.

MARCH TABLE

to accompany 146th Infantry Brigade Operation Order No.73.

Unit.	From.	To.	To pass Fort ROUGE at	To pass Point T.1i.a.7.9.Cross Roads in LaNIEPPE (Sht.27.) at	Route.
464th Coy. A.S.C.	ST MARTIN.	P.22.a.6.6.		10.30.a.m.	To move via CLAIRMARAIS and HAUT SCHONBROUCK PLATTE BEURRE and STAPLE.
1/5th Bn. W.York.R.	ST MARTIN.	Billets in ST MARIE CAPPEL.		10.40.a.m.	
1/6th Bn. W.York.R.	SAPERICK.	Tents in Camp at ST MARIE CAPPEL.		11.10.a.m.	
146th M.G.Company.	TATINGHEM.	U.18.d.5.5.	10.0.a.m.		via EBBLINGHEM. There is a good road from FORT ROUGE to RENESCURE,(not shown on map).
146th Brigade H.Q.	LONGUENESSE.	St MARIE CAPPEL.		10.10.a.m.	
1/7th Bn.W.York.R.	LONGUENESSE.	THERDINGHEM.		11.40.a.m.	To move via ARCQUES, PLATTE BEURRE and STAPLE. NOT to pass FORT ROUGE before 10.0a.m.
1/8th -do-	TATINGHEM.	OXELAERE.		12.10.p.m.	
146th T.M.Battery.	COPETTE.	P.21.c.0.1.		12.30.p.m.	
458th Field Coy. R.E.	COPETTE.	P.26.c.4.8.		12.35.p.m.	
1/1st Field Amb.	LONGUENESSE.	O.24.d.5.9.		12.45.p.m.	

Appendix B(1)

SECRET   Copy No. 4

146th INFANTRY BRIGADE OPERATION ORDER No.74.

2nd Oct.1917.

Ref. Maps Sheet 27, &
HAZEBROUCK 5.a.

1. 146th Infantry Brigade Group will move to WATOU No.2.area to-morrow, 3rd inst in accordance with accompanying March Table.

2. All halts will be at clock hour minus 10 minutes to clock hour.
   Long halt at 2.30.p.m. to 3.30.p.m. - optional for leading units (1/7th Bn.W.York.R., 146th Brigade H.Q. and 1/6th Bn.W.York.R.)

3. Usual distances to be maintained on the march.

4. 146th Brigade H.Q. office will be at L.13. central (tents).

5. ACKNOWLEDGE.

                                    W Fisher
                                           Captain,
                        Brigade Major, 146th Infantry Brigade.

Issued at 8.30.p.m.

Copy No.1.   1/5th Bn.W.York.R.
       2.   1/6th   -do-
       3.   1/7th   -do-
       4.   1/8th   -do-
       5.   146th Machine Gun Coy.
       6.   146th Trench Mortar Bty.
       7.   Staff Capt. 146th Brigade.
       8.   O.C.No.2.Signal Section
       9.   T.O. 146th Brigade.
      10.   458th Field Coy.R.E.
      11.   464th Coy. A.S.C.
      12.   1/1st Field Ambulance.
      13.   49th Division 'G'.
      14.   49th Division 'A' & 'Q'.
      15.   War Diary.
      16.   Retained.
      17.   "
      18.   File.

MARCH TABLE

to accompany 146th Infantry Brigade Operation Order No.74.

Unit.	From.	To.	Pass Starting Point.P.4.b.7.3. at	Route.
1/7th Bn.W.York.R.	TERDEGHEM.	L.14.	11.30.a.m.	STEENVOORDE – Road junction K.32.d.5.0 – RATTEKOT INN, K.16.b.8.8. – K.12.c.6.2.
146th Brigade H.Q.	ST MARIE CAPPEL.	L.13.central.	12. 0.noon.	
1/6th Bn.W.York.R.	–do–	L.13.	12.5. p.m.	
1/5th	–do–	L.2.&.L.7.b.	12.25.p.m.	
146th T.M.Battery.	P.27.c.4.9.	L.13.b.3.6.	12.45.p.m.	
1/8th Bn.W.York.R.	OXELAERE.	L.8.	1. 0.p.m.	(NOTE – The BAVINCHOVE – OXELAERE – QUAESTRAETE Road to be kept clear for other Brigades to pass from 8.0.a.m. onwards).
464th Coy. A.S.C.	P.22.a.6.6.	L.1.c.5.2.	1.20.p.m.	
458th Field Coy.R.E.	P.26.c.4.8.	L.7.b.1.4.	1.30.p.m.	
1/1st (W.R.)Field Amb.	0.24.b.5.0.	L.19.b.3.6.	1.40.p.m.	
146th M.G.Company.	U.18.d.5.4.	L.13.d.3.4.	2. 0.p.m.	

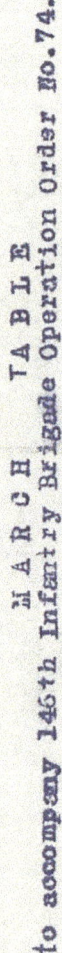

SECRET *Appendix B(ii)*   *War Diary*

1/8th. Bn. WEST YORKSHIRE REGIMENT
OPERATION ORDER NO. 48

October 2nd 1917.

Reference Map: HAZEBROUCK 5.A.   Sheet 27.

(1) **MOVE**

The Battalion will move by march route to WATOU No 2 Area (midway between WATOU & POPERINGE) to-morrow

Starting point Road Junction 250 yards N. of Battalion H.Q.

(2) **ROUTE**

ST. MARIE CAPPEL - TERDEGHEM - P.4.b.7.5. *and see below.*

(3) **ORDER OF MARCH**

Order of march H.Q., B, C, D, A, Transport.
Band will start with "B" Company, dropping back at each halt.
H.Q. will pass the Starting Point at **11-0** a.m.
100 yards interval will be kept between Companies and corresponding units.
"D" Company will join the Battalion on the MARIE CAPPEL road at nearest point to their own billets.

(4) **GENERAL**

Usual orders hold good as regards dress and march discipline.
2/Lieut. STUDLEY will be in charge of the rear party, and 1 Sergeant per Company will report to him at Starting Point.
2/Lieut. GARDNER will be in charge of slow party. Men already detailed will report to him at Starting Point at **11.0** a.m.
A Map will be provided for him.
Urgent cases of sick will be seen at 8.30 a.m.
The Transport Officer will arrange to collect kit, informing H.Q. and Companies what time transport will be there.
H.Q. Rations will be carried on "D" Coys Cooker
Band   "   "   "   "   "   "G" "   "

5 **Halts** Halts will be from ten minutes to the clock hour to the clock hour.
A long halt will be taken from 2-30 pm to 3-30 pm. Companies will arrange tea or such meal as they desire, to be ready at 2-30 pm.

(6) Route from Brigade S.P.   STEENVORDE - road junction K.32.d.50. RATTEKOT INN, K.6.b.8.8. - K.12.c.6.2. - L.8.

W M Brooke
Major.
Adjutant 1/8th. West Yorkshire Regiment.

Appendix C

SECRET   Copy No. 4

146th INFANTRY BRIGADE OPERATION ORDER No. 75.

5th Oct. 1917.

Ref Maps Sht.27.N.E.)
      "   28.N.W.) 1/40,000.

1. 146th Infantry Brigade (less one Battalion) will move to VLAMERTINGHE No.2.Area to-morrow, 6th inst - personnel by bus, transport by march route.

2. Billeting parties of 1/7th & 1/8th Bns.W.York.R., 146th Machine Gun Company, 146th Trench Mortar Battery to meet Staff Captain, 146th Inf.Brigade at Area Commandant's Office, VLAMERTINGHE at 10.0.a.m. 6th inst.

3. (a) Units will enbus in the following order :-

      146th Brigade H.Q.   4.30.p.m.
      1/7th Bn.W.York.R.   4.35.p.m.
      1/8th   -do-   5.5. p.m.
      146th Machine Gun Coy. 5.35.p.m.
      146th T.M.Battery.   5.45.p.m.
      Embussing point. K.17.b.5.8.

(b) Transports of units will move by march route immediately after mid-day meal under arrangements to be made by the Brigade Transport Officer. 500 yards distance to be maintained between transports of Battalions.

4. Completion of moves to be reported to Brigade H.Q.

5. 146th Brigade H.Q. Office will be in huts in No.2 Area about N8b.7.4.

6. ACKNOWLEDGE.

                                                                          Captain,
Issued at 9.0. p.m.   Brigade Major, 146th Inf.Brigade.

Copy No.1. 1/5th Bn.W.York.R.
     2. 1/6th -do-
     3. 1/7th -do-
     4. 1/8th -do-
     5. 146th Machine Gun Coy.
     6. 146th Trench Mortar Bty.
     7. Staff Capt. 146th Brigade.
     8. O.C.No.2.Signal Section.
     9. T.O.146th Brigade.
    10. 49th Division 'G'.
    11.   -do-   'A' & 'Q'.
    12. 464th Coy. A.S.C.
    13. Area Commandant, WATOU.
    14. War Diary.
    15. Retained.
    16. File.

NOTE: 1/5th Bn.W.York.R. moved to-day to VLAMERTINGHE.
       1/6th -do-   moved to-day to old British Front
                               line - transport G.S.c.

SECRET.   Appendix D   Copy. No. 4
                                                5th Oct. 1917.

ATTACK WEST OF PASSCHENDAELE.

146th INFANTRY BRIGADE INSTRUCTIONS No.1.

Reference Maps, POLYGON WOOD. 1/20,000.
              Sheet 20.S.E.3.)
                  " 28.N.E.1.) 1/10,000.

Stores, etc required for the attack.

1. In considering the quantity of various stores which will be required, the following points, the results of experiences of Divisions which have been fighting on this front will be borne in mind :-

   (a) The troops must go as light as possible, especially the front wave of the assault on each objective, and in our case the second objective will require the most active treatment.

   (b) One shovel to three men appears to have been sufficient; and if wet it will probably be best to dispense with these.
   Some Divisions have run short of S.A.A. during the fighting. All troops except the first wave for the assault on each objective should carry an extra bandolier.

   (c) Artificial obstacles have not been a cause of trouble, but on our second objective there may be patches of wire as it forms part of an organized trench system.

   (d) Positions of assembly will require to be most carefully marked out with tapes, and notice boards, showing the number of the platoon, thus

   These are being made.

   (e) Visual signalling has been of the greatest use and might be more fully employed.

   (f) It is not necessary to load the troops with an extra water-bottle to carry, but provision must be made for cold tea or water for them to drink at the position of assembly during the night so as to ensure their starting with a full bottle in the morning.

   (g) Very few bombs (hand) are required, and these only for clearing dug-outs. No difficulty has so far been experienced in this, but very few deep dug-outs have been encountered.
   There probably will be some in our second objective and there may also be the remains of trenches on our flanks.

   (h) Flares will be burnt at the long halts as well as on the final objective. They will not be burnt while troops are on the move.

Rifle Covers.

2. Rifle covers for keeping mud, etc., out of rifles must be tied on so that when the rifle is used they hang out

of the way clear of the rifle but will not get lost.

Pigeons.

Signal Communications. 3. (a) It is hoped that about 28 birds daily for the Brigade will be available. Pigeons will be collected by Brigade and Battalion pigeon men, who must work under the orders of the Brigade Signal Officer, from the most advanced point to which it is possible to get a motor-cycle D.R.

(b) <u>Visual</u> - The ground offers excellent prospects of Visual signalling with Lucas lamps, of which each Battalion now has four.

(c) ALL CIRCUITS laid during and after the attack must be metallic and only twisted cable must be used.

4. <u>ACKNOWLEDGE</u>.

Issued at ....   W.Fisher Captain,
                   Brigade Major, 146th Infantry Brigade.

Copy No. 1. 1/5th Bn. W.York.R.
       2. 1/6th   -do-
       3. 1/7th   -do-
       4. 1/8th   -do-
       5. 146th Machine Gun Coy.
       6. 146th Trench Mortar Bty.
       7. O.C. No.2 Signal Section.
       8. I.O. 146th Inf. Brigade.
       9. Retained.

SECRET.
                                        Copy No. 4.

ATTACK WEST OF PASSCHENDAELE.

186th INFANTRY BRIGADE   INSTRUCTIONS No.2.

1. CONSOLIDATION. -

   The position to be captured will be consolidated in depth, but the final objective will be held in such a manner and in such strength as to secure a good starting line for the next stage of the attack and the repulse of counter-attack on it. It must not in any way be looked upon as an outpost line.

2. LIAISON. -

   A Senior Officer of the Field Artillery will live with the H.Q. of each attacking Infantry Brigade.

   Field Artillery Liaison Officers will also be attached to the H.Q. of each assaulting Battalion.

3. S.O.S. -

   Artillery will only respond to the S.O.S. Signal for fifteen minutes and machine guns for eighteen minutes from the time the S.O.S. Barrage actually opens.

   The S.O.S. Signal must be repeated within five minutes of the end of the above periods if continuance of the S.O.S. barrage is required.

   Attention is called to II Anzac Artillery Instructions No.12, copy of which is attached.

4. CONTACT AEROPLANES.

   (i) (a) All contact work with troops of 2nd Anzac will be carried out by aeroplanes of 21st Squadron R.F.C.

   (b) Contact aeroplanes will be distinguished by one black streamer on each lower plane.

   (c) Machines of 21st Squadron R.F.C. carry the following distinguishing marks :-
   On fuselage, working from observer's seat towards rudder :-
   British markings.
   Large 'A' in white.
   A dumbell, painted in white.
   These markings are on both sides of the fuselage.

   (ii)   Only one contact aeroplane will work on the Corps front at one time.

   (iii)(a) Aeroplanes will call for flares at stated times by sounding a series of A's on the Klaxon Horn and by firing a white Very light.
   Ordinarily both signals will be used, but troops must be prepared to answer either, in the event of one of the signals breaking down.

   (b) Troops will be prepared to light flares at times other than above, if the aeroplane calls for them.

-2-

A special aeroplane may be ordered up by the Corps General Staff for this purpose.

(iv)   Flares No.3 RED will be used. These Flares are plainly visible and it is not necessary to light them in groups of two or three, as with the Green flare.
They are more easily distinguished, if lit at the bottom of a trench or of a shell hole.

(v)   1st Wave only is detailed to light flares so as to ensure that only advanced troops light them at the times referred to in para.R4(iii)

(vi)(a) The contact aeroplane will be fitted with wireless.
One wireless receiving set has been issued to each Division. It will be established at Headquarters of the Reserve Brigade.

(b) In addition to code messages laid down on page 71 of S.S.135, the following code will be used :-

ENEMY COLLECTING at .....   Succession of "Q's".
ENEMY ADVANCING FROM ....   Succession of "R's".
MORE THAN A BATTALION ...   LN
LESS than a BATTALION ...   SN

Message will be preceded by Squadron Call (FP) - Thus :- "Enemy collecting at B.6.a. more than a Battalion" would read :-
FPFPQQQB6aLN.

(c) O.O.C.Reserve Brigade will be responsible in the first instance for passing on all such messages to the two attacking Brigades of his Division and to his Division Headquarters.

5. RELIEFS. -

Machine Gun Companies on relief of Divisions will NOT accompany their Division, but will be concentrated into a Corps pool under Corps orders.

Divisions and Brigades on going into action again will be rejoined by their own machine gun units in accordance with their tactical requirements.

6. LIAISON. -

Major SYKES,M.C., 1/8th Bn.W.York.R. is detailed to report to 49th Divisional H.Q. for liaison purposes with flank Divisions,etc.

7. INTELLIGENCE. -

EXAMINATION OF PRISONERS.

Prisoners must not be delayed on the way to the Divisional Cage and on no account is an examination of prisoners or documents to be held except by the Officers authorised for the purpose by the General Staff.
Escorts should be cautioned to be on the look-out for Prisoners trying to throw away documents. One man of the escort should be detailed to march in the rear and see that no documents are thrown away.
The Divisional Intelligence Officer will be either at the forward or rear Divisional Cage and will be responsible for the forwarding of documents to the Corps Cage, labelled

with the prisoner's name.

SALVAGE.

1/6th Bn.W.York.R. will detail one responsible N.C.O. and each detail will detail one man, to report to the Brigade Intelligence Officer as early as possible, on arrival in VLAMERTINGHE No.1.Area, to collect documents from dug-outs and German dead, care being taken not to remove identity discs or soldbuch.

All documents obtained in this manner should be labelled stating where found and forwarded as quickly as possible to ~~Divisional H.Q.~~ Brigade H.Q.

The Intelligence Salvage men will wear white arm-bands which will be supplied by the Brigade. These men will be provided by with electric torches. All information available as to enemy headquarters,etc., will be notified to Salvage men by Brigade before commencement of operations.

INTELLIGENCE SUMMARIES.

On the Division taking over the line Battalion Summaries of Intelligence from six.a.m. to six.a.m. will be sent off so as to reach Brigade H.Q. by 8-30.a.m.

In active operations no summary need be compiled on attack day, but all intelligence will be sent by wire.

MESSAGE CARDS. -

Message cards are being prepared and 120 per Battalion will be issued. The importance of these cards being used should be impressed upon all ranks.

Message Cards have often proved to be the most useful in locating our own front line after successful operations.

8. TRACKS. -

Attached Map shows the tracks at present in use on the Divisional front.

9. ACKNOWLEDGE. -

                                                    Captain,
Brigade Major, 146th Infantry Brigade.

Issued at 7.p.m
5-10.17

Copy No. 1. 1/5th Bn.W.York.R.
        2. 1/6th   -do-
        3. 1/7th   -do-
        4. 1/8th   -do-
        5. 146th Machine Gun Coy.
        6. 146th Trench Mortar Bty.
        7. O.C.No.2 Signal Section.
        8. I.O. 146th Brigade.
        9. Retained.

II Anzac Corps R.A.205/1/27.G.

2nd ANZAC ARTILLERY INSTRUCTIONS No.12.
ARRANGEMENTS for S.O.S.

1. When an S.O.S. Signal is received, all barrages will go down on their protective Lines as indicated in Appendix *.

2. "A" Barrage will fire on their Protective Line at two rounds per gun per minute for fifteen minutes, and then cease fire.

3. B. C. D. E. Barrages will fire for two minutes on their Protective Lines and then creep forward for 500 yards by lifts of 100 yards every two minutes, jumping back to their Protective Lines for two minutes before ceasing fire.
   18-pdrs, will fire two rounds per gun per minute, other natures in proportion.

4. If no further message is then received, the Artillery barrage will cease, but "C" barrage will continue for a further three minutes.

5. If the S.O.S. signal or message is repeated within five minutes of the end of the above periods, the procedure will be repeated.

6. The above instructions are issued in order to avoid, as far as possible, any unnecessary expenditure of ammunition.

                         (sd) -   Major, S.C.R.A.
Oct.3rd 1917.   II Anzac Corps.

146th INF BRIGADE MAP No 25
SHOWING TRACKS
Not To Be Reproduced

REFERENCE
- Mule Track ....
- Duckboard Track (Double) ....
- " " Single ....
- Infantry " No Duckboards ....

— SECRET —

SCALE 1:20,000

S E C R E T.   Copy No. 4.

ATTACK WEST of PASSCHENDAELE.

146th INFANTRY BRIGADE INSTRUCTIONS NO. 3.

1.   The offensive will be resumed on X day in conjunction with the 148th Infantry Brigade on our right and a Brigade of the 48th Division on our left.

2.   Zero hour will be notified later.

3.   Objective lines RED and BLUE, Brigade and Battalion Boundaries and Barrage timings are shown on the attached Map. *(will follow →)*

   (a) The infantry will start from a tape line approximately one hundred and fifty yards from the opening barrage.

   (b) The RED and BLUE protective barrages are placed approximately two hundred yards in advance of the objectives to be consolidated, but all enemy strong points short of the protective barrage must be dealt with by the infantry.
        The line of the protective barrage has been placed so as to keep under fire strong points which are too far in advance of the line of consolidation to be dealt with by infantry.

4.   CONTACT AEROPLANES. -

   (a) Attention is drawn to 146th Brigade Instructions No. 2 para. 4.

   (b) Aeroplanes will call for flares at the following times:- on the RED line (intermediate objective) at Zero plus eighty minutes; on the BLUE line at Zero plus one hundred and seventy minutes.

   (c) An aeroplane will fly over the front line and will call for flares on the morning of Y day as early as weather conditions permit.

5.   ARTILLERY. -

   (a) Attention is called to this office No. 4/58.B., dated 5/10/17, and Table attached thereto.

   (b) As a signal to the infantry that the barrage has reached these lines, each 18-pdr. of barrage 'A' will fire Smoke Shell for a period of one minute on arriving on the 22 - 28 lift and on the 136 - 140 lift, and will also fire Smoke Shell for a period of five minutes on arriving on the RED and BLUE protective barrage lines.

   (c) If the wind is suitable a small amount of Smoke is to be fired in 'B' barrage throughout the advance.

   (d) C.R.A. will arrange for the whole of the advance to be screened by Smoke on the N.W. slopes of the PASSCHENDAELE Ridge and the Western edge of the village of PASSCHENDAELE.

-2-

6. CONSOLIDATION. -

(a) Attention is drawn to 146th Brigade Instructions No.2. Para.1.

(b) Strong points will be established at the following places :-

    148th Infantry Brigade -   D.11.a.3.8.
                                    D.4.d. .9.5.

    146th Infantry Brigade -   D.4.c.9.3.

7. The assaulting Battalions will move into their positions of assembly on the night W/X.

As each Company of the leading wave is completely in position, the Company of the 147th Infantry Brigade which is responsible for that area will be withdrawn.

147th Infantry Brigade will be assembled by Zero on the Southern slopes of the RAENSTAFEL - DEAR HO. HILL Ridge.

8. Instructions for Operations which may be carried out on X day wx subsequent to the capture of the BLUE line will be issued separately.

9. ACKNOWLEDGE.

                                                W Fisher Captain,
                                 Brigade Major, 146th Inf.Brigade.

Issued at .....p.m.

    Copy No.1. 1/5th Bn.W.York.R.
           2. 1/6th   -do-
           3. 1/7th   -do-
           4. 1/8th   -do-
           5. 146th Machine Gun Coy.
           6. 146th Trench Mortar Bty.
           7. O.C.No.2 Signal Section.
           8. I.O.146th Brigade.

SECRET.   COPY NO. 4..

ATTACK WEST of PASSCHENDAELE.

146th INFANTRY BRIGADE INSTRUCTIONS   NO.4.

7th Oct.1917.

1. All reconnoitring Officers and guides to reconnoitre No.6 Track and area.

2. 1/7th Bn.W.York.R. will assemble at LA BRIQUE
   1/8th   -do-   will assemble at ST JEAN - both by 9.a.m. 8th inst.

   146th M.G.Company.) will assemble at WIELTJE by 9-30.a.m.
   146th T.M.Battery)

3. Units will move up at dusk in the following order, to their assembly positions :-

   1/5th Bn.W.York.R. - to start about 5.p.m.) All to go
   1/7th   -do-   )
   1/8th   -do-   ) by
   146th M.G.Company (less 2 sections)   )
   146th T.M.Battery.   ) No.6 Track.
   1/6th Bn.W.York.R.   )

4. 146th Infantry Brigade Battle H.Q. will be at GALLIPOLI, D.13.d.8.2.

5. ACKNOWLEDGE.

                                      J W Fisher Captain,
                              Brigade Major, 146th Inf.Brigade.

Issued at .9.0.p.m.

   Copy No.1, 1/5th Bn.W.York.R.
         2.   1/6th   -do-
         3.   1/7th   -do-
         4.   1/8th   -do-
         5.   146th Machine Gun Coy.
         6.   146th Trench Mortar Bty.
         7.   O.C.No.2 Signal Section.
         8.   I.O.146th Brigade.
         9.   49th Division 'G'
        10.   Retained.

SECRET.   COPY NO. 4

146TH INFANTRY BRIGADE ADMINISTRATIVE INSTRUCTIONS. NO.1.

Reference Map Sheet 28. 1/40,000.   7th October, 1917.

1.   WATER.

   Care will be taken to salve all petrol and water tins.

2.   SUPPLIES.

(i). Railhead.   EDEWAARTHOEK.   G.5.a.

(ii). Refilling Point.   G.6.d.2.4.

(iii). Supplies will be drawn from Railhead by Divisional Train and delivered to units at transport or wagon lines. The Left Brigade deliver to Brigade Dump by horse transport; the Right Brigade by pack transport.

(iv). Rations.

   The following rations will be held :-

   (a). Iron rations on the man.
   (b). Current days rations.
   (c). 8,200 Preserved Meat and biscuit and solidified alcohol.

   Right Brigade - C.24.b.9.7.   4,000.
   Left Brigade - C.18.d.6.6.   4,000.
   Prisoners of War Cage.   200.
                                  8,200.

   (d). 6,000 dry rations held by O.C. 49th Divisional Train at the COLLEGE, POPERINGHE.

(v). A day will eventually be fixed for the consumption of the rations mentioned in para; 4 (d) and the balance will be effected by underdrawing at Railhead.
   Bacon and cheese will be drawn to supplement this ration when consumed.

3.   R.E. STORES.

(i). Railhead OAKHANGAR G.3.b.

(ii). The situation of R.E. Dumps is given below.

(iii). Stores will be supplied under arrangements to be made by C.E. with C.R.Es. concerned.

                             DUMPS.

   (a).   G.3.c. central.   Corps.
   (b).   H.8.a.5.9.   Main Divisional.
   (c).   WIELTJE.   Advanced Divisional.
   (d).   C.18.d.5.3.   Intermediate. (Left Brigade).

   Material may be drawn from any of the above mentioned Dumps on Indent signed by Commanding Officer or Adjutant.

- 2 -

4.   AMMUNITION SMALL ARMS, GRENADES, ETC.

(i). <u>Existing system of supply.</u>

Corps Sub Park delivers to Divisional Grenade Officer at the Divisional Dump by motor lorries. The Divisional Grenade Officer delivers to Brigade Officers by horse transport.

(ii). <u>Dumps.</u>

Left Brigade.	C.18.d.6.6.	Scattered both sides of road.
Right Brigade.	C.24.b.9.7.	Scattered both sides of mule-track.
Divisional.	I.3.a.	ST. JEAN.
M.G. S.A.A. DUMP.	C.24.a.3.6.	Bridge House.

(Personnel to be found by D.M.G.O.)

(iii). The following initial allotment of S.A.A., Grenades, Trench Mortars, Ammunition, and Fireworks is made :-
These quantities are additional to the authorised establishment and to the quantities carried on the man.
Demands to complete to allotment will be wired to this office on taking over and while in the line.

Detail.	Per Bde in Line.	Divisional Dump.
S.A.A.	1,000,000.	1,000,000.
Mills Hand Grenades.	3,000.	3,000.
Mills Rifle "	3,000.	3,000.
Rifle Grenades No. 22.	2,000.	2,000.
" " " 24.	2,000.	2,000.
T.M. 3" per mortar.	100.	40.
"P" Grenades,	500.	500.
No.27 Smoke. (a).	400.	400.
No.28 K.J. (b)	300.	300.
Smoke Candles - type S.	3,000.	3,000.
Flares No.3 Red.	5,000.	5,000.
S.O.S. Rifle Grenades (c).	200.	200.
Cartridges. D.I. 1½".	1,000.	1,000.
" " 1 ".	4,000.	4,000.
" Signal. 1½".	500.	500.
" " 1 ".	500.	500.
Daylight Mortar Signals.	30.	40.

(a). 25% rods are issued with these grenades; further rods in reasonable quantities can be obtained on demand.

(b). For use in clearing dug-outs - non-poisonous fumes which produce violent coughing. The German Gas Mask is not proof, but British Small Box Respirator is proof against them.

(c). Signal Parachutes - 3 lights; red over green over yellow.
     "   "   - White to green first.) change S.O.S.
     "   " 1½"- white red second) to be issued
) when necessary.

(iv). The authorised reserves of S.A.A. and Grenades carried on vehicles of units will be maintained correctly loaded and ready to move forward at short notice - if required.

3.

(v). Grenades will be detonated at the Divisional Dump before being sent forward to Brigade Dumps.

Brigades will detail one N.C.O. and 10 men each to report to Divisional Grenade Officer when required. These men to have a thorough knowledge in detonating.

(vi). The existing system at Divisional Dump will continue during operations, i.e.,

    3 Artillery Officers.
    30 Limbered Wagons.
    30 Artillery Personnel.

5.   CASUALTIES.

(i). Estimated Casualty reports will be rendered to Brigade Headquarters at the following times:-
                6.30 a.m.
                3.0 p.m.
and more frequently if considered necessary.

(ii). Such wires will not include any numbers previously reported; in all other respects the procedure laid down in Second Army Circular A.2528 pages 4 and 5 will be adhered to.

(iii). An accurate report will be rendered daily by 3 p.m. for the period noon to noon, and it is of the utmost importance that such returns be rendered as punctually and as accurately as possible.

(iv). Great care must be taken regarding the reporting of officers casualties. It is important that names are correctly given and that all initials are verified before being reported. Actual dates of all officer casualties must be given.

(v). Whenever a Battalion has lost 50 or more men "missing" in any single day, a foot-note will be added stating number believed to have been taken prisoners.

(vi). It is important that casualty reports be forwarded regularly and accurately.

6.   GENERAL.

(i). Additional ammunition etc., to be carried on the man can be drawn from ST. JEAN C.27.d.0.0. as follows :-

Each Battalion :-
    35,000 rounds S.A.A.
    1,000 grenades.
    50 S.O.S. Signals.
    1,000 Ground Flares.

(ii). Authority has also been obtained to draw 1,400 Sandbags and 600 Shovels if required from the R.E. Dump at WIELTJE.

(iii). Arrangements are being made for the formation of a more advanced Ammunition Dump but until this is formed supplies should be drawn from C.18.d.5.3.

7.   ACKNOWLEDGE.

                                                  Captain,

                Staff Captain, 146th Infantry Brigade.

COPIES TO :-

1. 1/5th Bn. Y. York R.
2. 1/6th   do.
3. 1/7th   do.
4. 1/8th   do.
5. 146th Machine Gun Co.
6. 146th Trench Mortar Battery.
7. 146th Bde. Transport Officer.
8. Quartermaster, 1/5th Bn. Y. York R.
9.   do.   , 1/6th   do.
10.   do.   , 1/7th   do.
11.   do.   , 1/8th   do.

Appendix E

CASUALTIES   1/8th BN WEST YORKSHIRE REGIMENT

Killed in Action 9-10-17

Lieut.Col. ROBERT ARTHUR HUDSON D.S.O.
Captain CHARLES JOHN CONSTABLE LA COSTE, M.C.
Captain ERIC FITZWATER WILKINSON, M.C.
Captain LESLIE WILFRED G. LLAGHAN
2/Lieut HAROLD NORTHROP
  "   ARTHUR LESLIE BAKER
  "   BASIL JAMES RICHARDSON
  "   CHARLES CARR STUDLEY

Wounded 9-10-17.

Captain HUGH RALPH LUPTON M.C.
Lieut. EDWARD CAULFIELD DUDGEON
2/Lieut ALBERT EDWARD ROLLS
2/Lieut WILLIAM HENRY BACKHOUSE
2/Lieut WILLIE GARDNER
2/Lieut FREDERICK THOMAS HUBAND WATKIN

L/M E.B. LEECH R.A.M.C.   Wounded & Remained at duty 9-10-17

Lieut REGINALD WALKER HORSFALL
Lieut. JOHN BUCKLEY.

Missing - 9-10-17.

2/Lieut WILLIAM METCALFE
2/Lieut ROBERT ORTON BOWRAN

A COMPANY.   Killed in Action 9-10-17.

305335 A/Sgt.Frankland.W.	305482 A/Sgt Jasper H
305406 A/Cpl.Marshall G.	307676 A/Cpl.Wells E
18/1096 L/Cpl Beach F	270081 Rfm Barker F wounded
307159 Rfm Blaymires J W	42828 " Cummings J G
48531 " Clarke H	205281 " Frankland.W.E
46080 " Greenwood T	48515 " Harker J.J
42898 " Kelly G	36997 " Lister E wounded
307808 " Murray G.S	48861 " Mannington.H
40918 " Morriss J.D	7108 " Moorfoot.M
307220 " Ramsey R	205142 " Rawson A
42876 " Smith G.S	54656 " Wilcock J.E

307321 A/Cpl Trotter

B COMPANY

258252 A/Sgt Walker E.	307726 Rfm Buckle P.
307557 Rfm Capes J.T	241879 " Dewhirst H
240587 " Hammond H	242076 " Keogh T
307257 Rfm Lane D.A	205176 " Priestley W.H
48737 " Scott G	48988 " Smith C.H
48732 " Varey E	

'C' COMPANY.

305664 Sgt.Limbert.G	305599 A/Cpl Jewitt
307760 A/Cpl.Fisher.J	305607 L/Cpl.Fletcher W.H
48398 Rfm.Crabbin G.	27638 Rfm Smith A
9765 " Shillshire C	5787 " Ward T

(continue

(continued)

'D' COMPANY.

34452 L/Cpl.Townsley.
307712 Rfm.Chadwick.J.W.
305508 "   Peacock.A.
305753 A/Cpl.Adams.G. ✓

Rfm
307156 Ex2Lt Broadbent.J.
 48576   "   Snagga.S.E.
305642   "   Wimbles.F.

Wounded - 9-10-17.

'A' COMPANY.

305601 Sgt.Flookton.J.
  9756 A/L/Sgt.Beattie.W.T.
  7550 A/Cpl.Larkin.J.
307698 Rfm.Maidens.S.
325135 L/Cpl.Taylor.W.
 42836 L/Cpl.Dale.C.W.
270094 Rfm.Boden.J.W.
 42834   "   Charlton.T.H.
 42894   "   Dean.J.
205040   "   Ibbotson.A.
325041   "   Owen.R.A.
 47287   "   Reid.E.
325087   "   Wells.C.E.

305839 A/Sgt.Wright.N.
307809 Sgt.Linfoot.R.
 41161 A/Cpl.Wilson.J.
306333 A/Cpl.Bowling.G.
 27476 A/Cpl.Martin.J.
307799 L/Cpl.Busfield.F.
 42829 Rfm.Clarkson.R.
306932   "   Carcaus.W.
 11949   "   Hughes.J.F.
 39744   "   Musgrove.J.E.
205193   "   Peckett.A.
305704   "   Smith.P.J.
 21446   "   Walker.R.

'B' COMPANY.

305813 Sgt.Mellor.W.
305831 A/Cpl.Hawes.E. ✓
306433 L/Cpl.Walker.H.
 39203 Rfm.Bell.E.
  9534   "   Carter.C.
205304   "   Fletcher.C.
266961   "   Howden.H.
 42866   "   Nicholson.J.
 54651   "   Reynolds.A.
325105   "   Simpson.J.
 42879   "   Scott.W.H.
307188   "   Steels.T.H.
242678   "   Whitton.J.H.

306035 Sgt.Coghill.D.   48732 Rfm.Douglas
307398 A/Cpl.Carter.C.A. 205146 - Bradshaw
 27586 Rfm.Butterell.C.E.
307282   "   Charlton.C.
 27409   "   Cowling.W.
307566   "   Gadsby.J.W.
 27655   "   Mawby.E.
 42872   "   Rowan.F.J.
305876 L/Cpl.Sykes.C.
325106 Rfm.Sawyn.G.
 42903   "   Sutton.R.W.
242177   "   Thackwray.H.
 42864   "   Morton
 42900   "   Tomlinson
 42308 L/Cpl Wilson

'C' COMPANY.

300098 A/Sgt.Hobson.H.
 46091 L/Cpl.Ottewell.
 21756 Rfm.Beaumont.J.
265726   "   Bradley.G.
306315   "   Colley.H.
242062   "   Drake.N.
 27614   "   Fowler.F.
203959   "   Higgins.J.
 26056   "   Jones.E.
 54653   "   Luke.T.
 54472   "   Mountain.J.A.
  8858   "   Marsland.J.
240684 L/Cpl.Parker.A.G.
 46112 Rfm.Ruddick.J.
 39349   "   Richardson.C.J.
270099   "   Sheldon.T.
 18391   "   Stretton.W.
202094   "   Tingay.B.
267454   "   Wrigglesworth.E.

307480 A/Cpl.Rothery.F.
203644 Rfm.Brear.H.
 32965   "   Brook.D.
 22810   "   Conboy.W.
 37080   "   Daniels.H.
 27610   "   Enwright.
 48845   "   Gill.J.H.
 42191   "   Hodgson.F.
 48989   "   Johnson.C.W.
  9451   "   Mitchell.J.
 48597   "   Mulvey.R.
306382   "   Mann.H.
 40649 L/Cpl.Pedley.G.
266894 Rfm.Row.J.
 47133   "   Softley.C.W.
203419   "   Savage.J.T.
277555   "   Thompson.W. sick
267449   "   Toes.W.C.T.

'D' COMPANY.

 22659 L/Cpl.Fellows.J.
307604 Rfm.Aram.F.
307711   "   Bradshaw.G.H.

  9584 L/Cpl.Strachan.A.
305520 Rfm.Birch.A.
 48488   "   Cornell.A.
207133 - Heywood

(continued)

(continued)   (3)

48897	Rfm.Cromack,H.	39480	Rfm.Dalby,A. *Died of wounds*
48572	" Easinwood,H.H.	307465	" Gibson,J.
48398	" Hutchinson,J.S.	307184	" Lemon,E.
306659	" Mack,F.	48574	" Matthews,G.H.
40932	" Moore,G.A.	15/1878	" Musgrave,.
267070	" North,J.	39785	" Newton,J.
325142	" Shuttleworth,W.	39558	" Sothcott,W.R
46504	" Smith,T.	43043	" Simmonite,J.
39524	" Stirk,F.W.	48610	" Turpin,W.
54562	" Watkins,W.J.	27460	" Whitfield,J.
24700	A/Sgt.Pickard,H.W.		

Missing 9-10-17.

'A' COMPANY.

42814	Rfm.Airay,C.H. *sick*	42816	Rfm.Beckett,H. *wounded not missing*
42818	" Burt,J.E	42692	" Burn,A.
307498	" Carter,J.B. *wounded not missing*	42832	" Clarke,F.W. *?S.W.*
42847	" Forest,E.	46078	" Furber,J.F.
42848	" Hogg,W.	270091	" Hulme,J.
39586	" Lonsborough,J.	307198	" Mason,W.
305178	" McKeating,J. *wounded, not missing*	37375	" Robinson,J.T.
205239	" Swanson,C.H.	241224	" Taylor,R.

'B' COMPANY.

9500	Sgt.Turner,E.	305519	A/Sgt.Ellie,J.H.
27482	A/Cpl.Bate,J. *wounded not missing*	307310	L/Cpl.Rablin,J.W
241603	Rfm.Adamson,S. *do.*	267489	Rfm.Baxter,J.
48739	" Barnes,J.	307438	" Constantine,J.
7996	" Foster,A.	48776	" Hall,E. *Wounded not missing*
307533	" Harker,H.O.	54548	" Lindsey,T.
267264	" Perrigo,M.	42878	" Smith,S.W.
42880	" Smith,A.E.	325144	" Simpson,M.
48749	" Selby,W.G. *do*	39646	" Whitney,H.
54655	" Watson,T. *Wounded not missing*		

'C' COMPANY.

267545	A/Sgt.Greenhough,H. *Wounded not missing*	27692	Rfm.Brogden,A.H. *Wounded not missing*
33188	Rfm.Bailey,S.	48990	" Beaumont,H.
267727	" Dobson,J.	48893	" Dunderdale,G.
267151	" Endley,T.A. *sick*	8390	" Francis,G. *Wounded not missing*
305903	" Ford,E. *sick*	305522	" Gaunt,L. *sick*
25255	" Goss,J.H.	307443	" Hepconstall,F. "
270066	" Hodson,H.	205058	" Hampson,A.
26584	" Jesson,F.	12/273	" Merry,L.W.
306769	" Marshall,G.W.	27447	" Pleasants,W.
48810	" Precious,F.	42423	" Rutter,C. *do*
27447	" Smithson,W.	270086	" Smith,A.
306697	" Scott,E.	39493	" Shaw,E.
270070	" Taylor,T. *do.*	205143	" Wilbur,J.
305815	" Wetherill,J.		

'D' COMPANY

19221	A/Sgt.Falkingham,F	8769	Sgt.Williams,J.D
307419	A/Cpl.Hall,G.E.	4/19861	Cpl.Hart,C.E
48578	L/Cpl.Webb,F.W.	48544	Rfm.Alexander,J.
306400	L/Cpl.Blakey,W.	49009	" Barrow,A.S.
307610	Rfm.Carter,F.	48653	" Coggins,W.
40597	" Davis,H. *Wounded not missing*	305279	" Evans,G.
266123	" Emmett,W.	307076	" Frankland,G
305216	L/Cpl.Greasley,S.	48618	" Gaffigan,J.G
38380	Rfm.Green,S. *do*	23866	" Hawe,A.
48574	" Hatfield,W. *do*	268856	" Hargreave,W.

(continued)

(continued) (4)

59560	Rfm Harrison.J.	48600	Rfm.King.A.	Wounded not missing
266361	" Meltz.M. Wounded not missing	270092	" Marsh.H.	
266332	" Mosley.H.	205306	" Marsden.S.	Wounded not missing
48820	" Martin.G.	307806	" Norland.N.	
48692	" Ramsden.H.	29785	" Squires.T.	
48784	" Scarth.J.G.	21710	" Taylor.W.	
307367	" Warner.J.W.	306861	" Wood.J. sick	
305313	" Woodward.G.H. do.	305312	" Wildcock.A. do	
27180	" Westfield.W.	54867	" Wheeler.J.	
54566	" Williams.W.H. do.	54564	" Williams.W.E.	
54560	" Walford.T.C.	42369	L/Cpl.Westhead.J. sick	
7078	A/Sgt.Woodward.G.J.			

Wounded and Missing 9-10-17.

'A' COMPANY.

40609 Rfm.Powell.J.W.

Missing believed killed 9-10-17.

'B' COMPANY.

256466 Rfm.Greenside.B.   16/1196 Rfm.Holdsworth.G.A. *Wounded not missing*

Wounded - Remained at duty 9-10-17.

"A" COMPANY.

6548 Rfm.Klar.A.W.   27706 Rfm.Webb.S.
305063 " Wright

"B" COMPANY.

305433 Sgt.Spencer.M.   307669 L/Cpl.Harper.R.
49300 Rfm.Richardson.F.G.

"C" COMPANY.

307397 A/Cpl.Buck.   305524 L/Cpl.Cullingworth.
14313 Rfm.Hopkinson.   9946 Rfm.Gledhow
243168 " Haynes.   240100 " Gilfoil
305094 " Avery.G.W.

"D" COMPANY.

267435 Sgt.Pawson.W.   48609 Rfm.Hoyle.C
305507 Rfm.Smith.T.

Wounded 9-10-17. Attached Brigade H.Q.

305837 L/Cpl.Ibbotson.W. D.Coy.   305199 Rfm.Wright.H. C.Coy.
46141 Rfm.Pringle.W. C.Coy.

Missing 10-10-17. Attached Brigade H.Q.

307694 Rfm.Myers.J.   D.Coy.

S E C R E T.   Appendix F   COPY NO. 4

146th INFANTRY BRIGADE OPERATION ORDER No. 78.

11th October 1917.

Ref Maps Sheets 28 N.W. and 27.

1. 146th Infantry Brigade and 464th Company A.S.C. will proceed to WINNIZEELE No.3 Area tomorrow 12th inst, - personnel by bus, transport by march route.

2. Embussing point, on the NEW YPRES - VLAMERTINGHE ROAD, at H.5.c.0.4. - head of column facing West.

3. Personnel of Units will embus as follows :-

146th Brigade H.Q. and)	
148th Brigade rear party) -	2- 0 p.m.
1/5th Bn. W.York. R.	2- 5 p.m.
1/6th do.	2-20 p.m.
1/7th do.	2-35 p.m.
1/8th do.	2-50 p.m.
146th Machine Gun Coy.	3- 5 p.m.
148th Machine Gun Coy.	3-10 p.m.
146th Trench Mortar Bty.	3-15 p.m.

4. 464th Company A.S.C. will start at 9-0 a.m.
   Transports of Units will start at 11-0 a.m. from Transport lines under orders of 146th Brigade Transport Officer, and proceed by POPERINGHE - Road junction L.13.d.6.0. - Road junction K.5.b.0.9. - WATOU.
   Cookers, under an Officer, may be sent on later if desired.

5. Billeting parties will proceed in advance and meet the Staff Captain, 146th Infantry Brigade, at Area Commandant's Office, WINNIZEELE, at 9-30 a.m.

6. ACKNOWLEDGE.

                                          Captain,
Issued at ... p.m.   Brigade Major, 146th Infantry Brigade.

   Copy No. 1. 1/5th Bn. W.York.R.
        2. 1/6th   do.
        3. 1/7th   do.
        4. 1/8th   do.
        5. 146th Machine Gun Coy.
        6. 146th Trench Mortar Bty.
        7. Staff Capt, 146th Bde.
        8. O.C.No.2.Signal Section.
        9. 146th Bde. Transport Officer.
       10. 49th Division, 'G'.
       11.   - do -   'A' & 'Q'.
       12. War Diary.
       13. Retained.
       14. File.

SECRET   Copy No 11

Appendix G.

1/8th BN. WEST YORKSHIRE REGIMENT

OPERATION ORDER NO. 43

Reference Map.   October 27th 1917
   Sheet 27 1/40,000. Special Map.

(1) **MOVE**

The Battalion will move by march route to STEENVOORDE EAST on the 28th inst.

(2) **ORDER OF MARCH**

Battalion will parade ready to move off at 8.05 a.m. and will move in order A. B. C. D. H.Q. Transport.
Band will start with A. and drop back one Company each halt. Halts will be as usual and usual distance will be maintained between Companies.
ROUTE. N 8.6 V.C. (Brigade S.P.) — STEENVOORDE

(3) **KITS**

All spare kits must be taken to Quarter Masters Stores to-night.

Blankets will be TIGHTLY rolled in bundles of 10, securely fastened and labelled. Time and place for dumping will be notified later.
Transport Officer will notify O.C. Companies, when and where Officers Valises and Mess Boxes are to be stacked.

(4) **REAR PARTY**

H.Q. and each Company will detail 1 Pioneer to report to Lieut BUCKLEY as rear party. This in no way absolves Companies and H.Q. from leaving their lines clean.

(5) **BILLETING PARTY**

Each Company and Transport Section will detail Q.M.Sergt to report to Lieut SHELLY at Orderly Room at 8.0.a.m. to act as Billeting Party.
They will obtain Bicycles at Q.M. Stores.

(6) **DISCIPLINE**

Strict march discipline will be maintained.

(7) **PACK PONIES**

Pack Ponies will be with Companies and H.Q.

                                                    W H Biddle
                                                    Major & Adjutant.
                                                    1/8th Bn. West Yorkshire Regiment

Copy No 1   C.O.
         2   Adjutant.
         3   O/C A Coy.
         4   " B "
         5   " C "
         6   " D "
         7   Medical Officer
         8   Transport Officer.
         9   Quartermaster.
        10   File.
        11   WAR DIARY.
        12   Retained.

On His Majesty's Service.

Vol 27

WAR DIARY
NOVEMBER 1917
1/8 WEST YORKSHIRE REGT

WAR DIARY / INTELLIGENCE SUMMARY

Army Form C. 2118.

1/2 West Yorkshire Regt

Place	Date	Hour	Summary of Events and Information	Remarks and references to Appendices
STEENVOORDE	Nov 1		The Divisional Commander inspected the Battalion at Training.	
"	2		A quiet day nothing to report	
"	3		A quiet day.	
"	4		Church Parades & Inspections. Major Brooke M.C. assumed the duties of 2ᵢ/c in command and Lieut Milligan became A/Adjutant.	
"	5		A quiet day. Training continued.	
"	6		Wet weather interfered with Training	
"	7		Training & Preparations for move	
"	8		The Battalion moved by bus to H.24.c.4.4. (Sheet 28) into huts.	
"	9		Reconnaissance of support Battn. position carried out by C.O. & Coy Commanders	
H.24.C.4.4	10		Preparations complete for moving into support position	
"	11		The Battalion moved into support position HQ at J.9.a.5.3. 2/Lieut Taft joined	
J.9.a.5.3.	12		A quiet day except for shelling. Lieut Hutchinson joined.	
	13		Seven casualties in O.R. and 2 OFFICERS all gassed. 1 O.R. wounded.	
	14		Much Shelling including gas shells causing some casualties	
	15		The Battn relieved the 1/7 Bn in the front line HQ at J.14.a.8.6.	

Army Form C. 2118.

WAR DIARY
INTELLIGENCE SUMMARY.
(Erase heading not required.)

1/3 East Yorkshire Regt.

Instructions regarding War Diaries and Intelligence Summaries are contained in F. S. Regs., Part II. and the Staff Manual respectively. Title pages will be prepared in manuscript.

Place	Date	Hour	Summary of Events and Information	Remarks and references to Appendices
Sead 28 J.4.a.8.6	Nov 16		A quiet day. Patrolling at night	
	17		The Battalion captured five prisoners	
	18		The Battalion captured two further prisoners.	
	19		The Battalion was relieved by the 1/6 Duke of Wellington Rl & moved into support at I.15.c.2.6.	
I.15.c.2.6.	20		The Battalion was relieved by the 1/6 Y.O.L. & moved into Reserve at WALKER CAMP.	
H.29.6.3.6	21/24		Four days were spent in training especially Lewis Gunners, Bombing & Musketry.	
			Up after the sharp review in the Front line on the 24th the Battalion was honoured by a visit from Major General Lord SCARBOROUGH, & Brig. General AMENDS Ron Col of the LEEDS RIFLES.	
H.23.c.6.9	25		The Battalion moved to a new camp at H23 c 69 in order to pursue working parties.	
	26/27		Working parties to the extent of 440 O.R. were found by the Battalion, and to help out our Coy of 70 O.R. was attached from the 1/6 West Yorkshire.	
I.13.6.9	28		At 5:30 p.m. the Battalion (along with the rest of the Brigade) moved into Divisional support at I.13.6.2.9. The move was completed without incident.	

Army Form C. 2118.

WAR DIARY
INTELLIGENCE SUMMARY.
(Erase heading not required.)

1/8 WEST YORKSHIRE REGT

Place	Date	Hour	Summary of Events and Information	Remarks and references to Appendices
	1917			
1361.29	Nov 29		Battalion supplies working parties amounting to 400 O.R. to C.O. and company commanders reconnoitred front line areas.	
	30		Morning parties to the extent of 300 O.R. were furnished. Desultory shelling of the built up place on Nov 29th and 30th but no casualties.	
			The following reinforcement of officers arrived on the 24 Nov. 2nd Lieuts HEFFERON, JEWITT, BARNETT, HARRISON, OLIVER, MIDGLEY, OATES, and S. BAILEY.	
			Casualties for November 1917	
			Killed in action — Officers — O.R. 11	
			Died of Wounds — 1 " 4 "	
			Wounded 5 " 52 "	
			Comparison of strength 1.11.17 32 officers 730 O.R.	
			30.11.17 35 officers 648 O.R.	
			Total 22 " 622 "	
			Ration 26 " 488 "	

M.K. Morgan Lieut Adjt
1/8 West Yorkshire Regt

Vol. 28

28 C
5 sheets

On His Majesty's Service.

War Duty

1/8th West Yorkshire Regiment

Army Form C.-2118.

WAR DIARY
INTELLIGENCE SUMMARY.
(Erase heading not required.)

1/8 West Yorkshire Regt

Place	Date	Hour	Summary of Events and Information	Remarks and references to Appendices
INFANTRY BARRACKS YPRES	Dec 1		The Battalion were in Divisional Reserve and provided working parties	Map Ref BELGIUM & FRANCE Sheet 28. 1/40000
	2		As above. Nothing to report	
	3		As above. Five reinforcement Officers reported for duty	
	4		Officers reconnoitred Brigade Support position.	
	5		The Battalion moved into Brigade Support at GARTER POINT	
GARTER PT	6		Carrying and working parties	
"	7		As above, some shelling	
"	8		As above, a quiet day.	
"	9		The Battalion relieved the 1/7 West Yorkshire Regt in the front line	
"	10		A quiet day, some shelling.	
	11		The Battalion was relieved by 1/5 D.of W.Rt. and moved into YPRES BARRACKS	
BARRACKS	12		The Battalion moved into Divisional Reserve at VANCOUVER CAMP.	
VANCOUVER CAMP	13		Employed on working parties and training	
"	14-16		As above	
"	17		The Battalion moved into BRIGADE RESERVE at DRAGOON CAMP relieving 1/7 D.of W.Rt.	
DRAGOON CAMP	18		Engaged on working parties	

Army Form C. 2118.

WAR DIARY
INTELLIGENCE SUMMARY.
(Erase heading not required.)

1/7 WEST YORKSHIRE REGT

Place	Date	Hour	Summary of Events and Information	Remarks and references to Appendices
DRAGOON CAMP	1917 Jan 22		The Battalion continued to supply working parties for the forward area	
	23		Relieved the 17 West Yorkshire Regt in the trenches on the 23rd inst. Fairly quiet. Wiring was greatly hindered owing to the frost	
	26	24 hrs	At 1 a.m. a party of 6 of the enemy attempted to raid one of the front line posts. They were driven off, leaving 1 man (51 R.I.R) dead. Three of the posts were wounded by bombs	
	27/28		A large number of gas shells were sent over and there was intermittent shelling throughout the day & night	
CHATEAU BELGE	29		The Battalion was relieved by the 1/5 of the W. Riding carried out without incident. Battalion moved into Divisional Reserve area at CHATEAU BELGE	
	30/31		All of the Battalion out on working parties. On the 31st the men of the Battalion had their Xmas dinner, most being from the 23rd inst on account of being in the line. N.C.Cliff copy Lt Col. comdg. trophy.	

Army Form C. 2118.

WAR DIARY
INTELLIGENCE SUMMARY.

(Erase heading not required.)

1/8 WEST YORKSHIRE REGT

Place	Date	Hour	Summary of Events and Information	Remarks and references to Appendices
CHATEAU BELGE	1917 Dec 31		Casualties for Dec 1917	
			Killed in action — Officers 0 R 5	
			Died of Wounds — " 2	
			Wounded — " 9	
			Returned to duty — " 3	
			Missing believed killed — " 1	
			Strength	
				1st Dec 1917 31st Dec 1917
			Total Strength 35 Officers 648 OR 41 Off. 659 OR
			Ration " 26 " 487 " 25 " 524 "
				Off i/c 1st/8 W Yorks Regt
				1st/8 West Yorkshire Regt